ETHICS, PRINCIPLES, AND LOGIC

JOHN HENRY WADLEY III, PH.D

authorHOUSE®

AuthorHouse™
1663 Liberty Drive
Bloomington, IN 47403
www.authorhouse.com
Phone: 1-800-839-8640

First published by AuthorHouse 12/30/2009

ISBN: 978-1-4490-5905-7 (sc)

Library of Congress Control Number: 2009913561

Printed in the United States of America
Bloomington, Indiana

This book is printed on acid-free paper.

CONTENTS

INTRODUCTION

Whence the day that we arrive at a controlled society, wherein man believes that he has the right to control the lives of the multitude, who gave him the rights of such powers? willingly or otherwise, if the multitude had any indication that their lives would result in the degradation, in what is considered a civilized world, of human essentials to live and thrive, they would not have signed up for such. In a world where civilization is determined by the action, and conditions of the people, their customs, traditions, virtues, values, morals, etc., there exists an underlying factor that dictates whether or not the civilization is, truly civilized. What is this underlying factor? Simply, "It's Ethics". "Ethics", is defined as: "The principle of right or good conduct or body of such principle". The problem here is that, although ethics has it's place value within our society, and among our individual households, who is it that determines what is ethical, and what is not? We like to believe that the people of a given society possesses the exact "Ethical Application" among their daily lives, and endeavors, however, it is unfortunate to note that, this is not the case; what may be ethical to one or a group of individuals. May not be the same to other individuals or groups. For instance, the ideological underpinnings of ethical dispensation from a political standpoint of republicans, is by far and largely contrary to Those of democrats, Or are they? Some would argue that they are only different in the public view thereby allowing the multitude to choose one or other; sort of like "Choosing the lesser of the two evils", since behind closed doors, they are Influenced by the exact same ethics and principles. This is the Pros, and Cons of politics. In truth it is more so the Pros doing the cons. The further misfortune here, is that, we are predisposed to select either one side or the other.

A continued evaluation of human beings, and human behavior, has led to an understanding of the apparent nature that we have to become congruent with those of like minds to contribute the necessities to effectuate the changes that are so badly needed. Keep in mind that religion has a purpose, insofar as ethics are concerned, hence principles. A great many rely on their religious beliefs to garner a significant measure of ethical application and fortitude, wherein the underlying factor contains the principles that's necessary to overcome the constraints that hinders endurance. For one aspect of human nature is to endure. To thrive amidst circumstances that prevent growth and development. Humanity grapple with the ideal of change, simply because change appears indicative of emotional displacement or mental instability, and overall disenfranchisement. For change seemingly constitute for most an up footmen of the every day consistency, and disrupts their sadly illusory ideal harmonious existence. For all of our life forces are utilized to maintain such accustomed harmony, wherein our ethics and principles are our treatment in this maintenance.

But are those really sound ethics, and principles we retort so freely? The guiding force that keeps everything welded! and, What are true "Principles"?

Principles are defined as: A broad and basic rule of truth; and should be so regarded as a foundation implement on our daily lives. The Ancients of old particularly those of ancient Egypt had the worlds most endearing philosophers. Herms Trismegistus, wrote in his philosophical parlances "Treats of Principles", by the numeral of seven (7) known as the seven (7) Hermetic Principles: (mind, correspondence, vibration, polarity, rhythm, cause, and effect, and generation).

1) Mind: All is mind, ever thing is energy. The universe is mental.
2) Correspondence: As it is above, so it is below, as it is below, so it is above.
3) Vibration: Nothing is stationary, everything vibrates.
4) Polarity: Every thing is double. Ever thing has its opposite. Extreme meets.
5) Rhythm: All is ebb and flow, action and reaction, advance and recoil.
6) Cause and Effect: Nothing happens by chance. Everything happens according to law.
7) Generations: Generations is manifest in every thing. Every thing is masculine and Feminine.

The careful study of these principles is a true master key for opening the door to all Knowledge. Nature hides in her bosom the greatest secrets of life. Logic is defined as: what is exact? valid and rational reasoning. That which is reasonable. All of which is indicative of application. It is in this said application that dictates of understanding is determined. Though it can be argued that one persons principles is not necessarily the next. Nor one persons view of logic and /or reason refuses to qualify for the next. However, the contention is not all possess the same ethics, principles, and logic. The requirements for meriting a qualitative and heightened sense of clear direction regarding judgment. Good sound judgment regarding interactions and decision making with strong mental and physical dynamics entice growth and development. The one thing that continues to crop up in the disillusionment of society lies in the state of mind seemingly inherent within the mental confines of the masses would do us well to always remember that limited thinking leads to limited actions, and limited actions in this country is a waste of time. If there is no progress then growth or development necessitate productivity. The concept has become "surrender or die". We must use methods better unspoken, after all to understand this reality in contrast it is Applicable to study and examine all these concepts from a philosophical stand point. Since every concept, thought, idea, conclusion, derives its foundation from philosophy. Then, and only then can we better serve ourselves, family and society.

PHILOSOPHY DEFINED

Philosophy above all is the contemplation and discussion of all things seen and unseen, their relationships, including their nature, cause and purpose, and their source. This contemplation, when strictly mental, oral or written (it should be noted that words and writing / action are thoughts expressed) is a science in its truest form. Philosophy begins with the obvious, and then systematically strips away all that is secondary until the primary is all that remains. It is only the philosopher who is able to perceive the subtle secondary from the true primary. Philosophy begins with the recognition of the sublime within the mundane.

PHILOSOPHY ITS MEANING AND ORIGIN

"O Philosophy, life's guide! O searcher-out of virtue and expeller of vices! What could we and every age of men have been without thee? Thou hast produced cities; thou hast called men scattered about into the social enjoyment of life."

These words written by the great Roman statesman, orator, and philosopher Cicero approximately 100 years before the Common Era are no less potent today as when they were first penned. Since time immemorial, philosophy has been loved by great thinkers and yet scorned and hated at times by the religious establishment.

The great wise men of ancient times were called sages or masters. These men (and sometimes women) of no ordinary intellect were referred to as "Those who know." Perhaps the most eminent of these ancient thinkers was the awe inspiring Pythagoras, born sometime between 600 and 590 BC. Due to his humility, instead of calling one of "Those who know," he coined the word philosopher, which he defined as "one who is attempting to find out." Pythagoras was certainly not the first "philosopher," but one of the first great thinkers to be known as a philosopher.

If we are to look to the legend for the origins of philosophy, the myth that its proponents allege is the oldest of all stories, is memorialized in Genesis chapter three. There we see Adam and Eve seeking knowledge and wisdom, the first philosophers.

"Now the snake was the most cunning animal that the Lord God had made. The snake asked the woman, 'Did God really tell you not to eat fruit from any tree in the garden?'"

"We may eat fruit of any tree in the garden," the woman answered, "except the tree in the middle of it. God told us not to eat the fruit of that tree or even touch it; if we do we will die."

The snake replied, 'That's not true; you will not die. God said that because he knows that when you eat it, you will be like God and know what is good and what is bad.'

The woman saw how beautiful the tree was and how good it's fruit would be to eat, and she thought how wonderful it would be to become wise. So she took some of the fruit and ate it. Then she gave some to her husband, and he also ate it. As soon as they had eaten it, they were given understanding... [Gn 3:1-7, Good News translation, American Bible Society, 1992]

Man has been seeking wisdom and understanding ever since. In this paper we do not need to address any possible theological teaching of the above (i.e. "Is the snake really a snake or an allegorical symbol of man's lower nature?" or "what does this story tell us about God's relationship to man?"). Those questions are for theology and religion to answer.

Religion and philosophy were not always separate and distinct disciplines. Rather, at one time they were inextricably intertwined. Arguably, the greatest of all philosopher priests was the Egyptian known by the Greeks as Hermes Mercurius Trismegistus. The title of "Thrice Great" was given to Hermes because he was said to be the greatest of all priests, the greatest of all philosophers, and the greatest of all kings. This philosopher priest was known in ancient Egypt as "Thoth" or "Djhuty," and was represented by the hieroglyph of a man's body with the head of an Ibis. To the Egyptian, Thoth was the personification of universal wisdom, the inventor of writing and the recorder of time. He is said to have revealed medicine, chemistry, law, art, astrology, music, rhetoric, magic, philosophy, geography, mathematics, anatomy, oratory to mankind. Some even attest that Hermes was known as Enoch, the great Jewish priest of antiquity.

Philosophy and religion were known as two sides of the same coin until Pythagoras more formally defined these subjects. He formulated the "Pythagorean Theory Of Triads." In this theory, the great orders of knowledge were represented by an equilateral triangle with philosophy at the apex, science in the lower left corner and theology/religion in the lower right. By this diagram, Pythagoras was representing what is now known as the Pythagorean Theory of Triads. He taught that the triangle was the skeleton of the universe.

Philosophy being at the apex was the highest of the three and the closest to the source, the indescribable space that religion most often calls God. Although science and religion are "lower" than philosophy, they sit at the foundation of the triangle and true science and true religion support philosophical thought.

Through science, the mind may be opened to the majesty and order of the universe. It is the science of astronomy that instructs us on the awe inspiring magnitude of the physical reality. Man then sees his body and personality as a mere spec on a piece of miniscule dirt we call Earth within a solar system that barely rates a footnote compared to the Milky Way Galaxy, which in itself is merely one of billions of galaxies.

It is through the gift of Philosophy that the true thinker, standing in reverent awe of the physical Reality, looks within and sees the transcendent inner Reality that encompasses the manifested and un-manifested, with the un-manifested a far superior and greater Reality than the outer physical universe. It is only through philosophy that man may begin to contemplate the majesty of the trueness of what lies within. Science however, ignites the sparks of contemplation, which is the springboard that allows the individual, through philosophy to land on the top of the vault of true reality.

Astronomy, with the Hubble Telescope and vast radio telescopes, can not help but to stretch the imagination of all but the walking dead. Fanned by the great wind of awe from science such as Biology, Music, and Physics, it is inevitable that the awakened thinker steps over the line from the mundane into the realm of philosophy. Science is to be embraced, not as an end in itself but rather a means to an end. To be certain, there are those who believe that science is a study of all that exists. This type of thinking is a rather late corruption of the discipline of science. The tragedy of meteoric rise of science and technology is the death of philosophy in most great minds of science.

However, note the commonality in the definition of philosophy as presented by twelve great philosophers.

> "The science of things divine and human, and the causes in which they are contained." (Cicero)
> "The science of effects by their causes." (Hobbes) "The science of sufficient reasons." (Leibnitz)
> "The science of things possible, inasmuch as they are possible." (Wolf)
> "The science of things evidently deduced from the first principles." (Descartes)
> "The science of truths, sensible and abstract." (de Condillac) "The application of reason to its legitimate objects." (Tennemann)
> "The science of the relations of all knowledge to the necessary ends of human reason." (Kant)

"The science of the original form of the ego or mental self." (Krug)
"The science of sciences." (Fichte)
"The science of the absolute." (von Schelling)
"The science of the absolute indifference of the ideal and real." (von Schelling)
"The identity of identity and non-identity." (Hegel)

See, Sir William Hamilton, lectures on metaphysics and logic; Boston, 1865.

The above definitions may be summarized to philosophy as the science of establishing the relationship between the things visible to their ultimate nature and cause. Modern science can be an invaluable tool for the philosopher's work toward accomplishing this goal, even if the "scientist" is oblivious to the philosophic ramifications of his work.

The other corner of the foundation of the Pythagorean Theory of Triads is theology/religion. According to Pythagorean, true religion should support one's philosophical endeavors. Therefore, religion should not be an end in and of itself, but a tool of the philosopher. Sadly, religion has become a universe unto itself with little but distain for the noble philosopher. The splitting off of religion from philosophy dates back to the early Christian era. Whether this split and religious contempt for philosophy was due to an attempt by the priests to gain absolute power over the masses, or a matter of ignorance, we can only speculate.

The early Christian Mystics were philosopher priests in the truest sense of the term. The early Christian mysteries and the well established philosophical Pagan mysteries had much in common and little aversion for each other.

In early Christian times, the most prominent of the Pagan philosophic mysteries as the rites of Mithras. In the first century B.C., the Persian philosophic mysteries, carried by conquest and trade found its way into Southern Europe and was quickly accepted and embraced by the subjects of Rome. The cult grew rapidly, especially among the Roman Legions, who carried the mysteries to all parts of Europe. As with the Egyptian mysteries (per Imblichus) and the Greek mysteries (per Plutarch), the mysteries of Mithras apparently consisted of three degrees with the first degree consisting of seven levels or steps.

During the first century A.D., the Mithraic Mysteries and Christianity co-existed without apparent animosity. In fact both schools of thought blended with each other and borrowed doctrine and rites. The following description of the Mithraic Mysteries appears as if one is describing Christianity:

> "... the identification of the object of adoration with light and sun; the legends of the shepherds with their gifts of adoration, the flood, and the ark; the representation in art of the fiery chariot, the drawing of water from the rock; the use of bell and candle, holy water and communion; the sanctification of Sunday and the 25th of December; the insistence on moral conduct, the emphasis placed on abstinence and self-control; the doctrine of heaven and hell, of primitive revelation, of mediation of the Logos (Word) emanating from the Divine, the atoning sacrifice, the constant warfare between good and evil and the final triumph of the former, the immortality of the soul, the last judgment, the resurrection of the flesh and the fiery destruction of the universe ..." [Id., (quoting the "Encyclopedia Britannica")]

With such commonalities, it may seem strange that such extreme hatred of the Pagan philosophic Mysteries by the Christian cult was manifested. The most likely reason for this divide was created by the church hierarchy in an effort to control the minds and every aspect of their subjects. The need for power and control by these individuals caused the deterioration of the true Christian faith. These men took the high and pure philosophic teachings of the Master Jesus the Christ and reduced them to a mere shadow of the true teachings of virtue and integrity as requisites for salvation.

It was in response to this deviation from the high moral teachings of the Master to a prosaic non-philosophic cult that promised easy salvation even to the most brutish, that the ire of the great philosopher Celsus was raised. Without bowing to political correctness and tenderness, Celsus wrote the following ardent criticism of what Christianity had become:

> "That I do not, however, accuse the Christians more bitterly than truth compels, may be conjectured from hence, that the criers who call men to other [philosophic] mysteries proclaim as follows: 'Let him approach whose hands are pure, and hose words are wise.' And again, others proclaim: 'Let him approach who is pure from all wickedness, whose soul is not conscious of any evil, and who leads a just and upright life.' And these things are proclaimed by those who promise purification from error. Let us now hear who those are that are called to the Christian Mysteries: Whoever is a sinner, whoever is unwise, whoever is a fool, and whoever, in short is miserable, him the Kingdom of God will receive. Do you not, therefore, call a sinner, an unjust man, a thief, a housebreaker, a wizard, one who is sacrilegious, and a robber of Sepulchers? What other persons would the crier nominate, who should call robbers together?" (Celsus)

With such animosity on both sides, it is no wonder that divide between philosophy and Christianity became the canyon that it is today. However, not all became the canyon that it is today. Religions are hostile to philosophy. The ultimate goal of religion is "salvation." As indicated hereinafter, Buddhism, Hinduism and Christian Gnosticism has little to no conflict philosophy. Judaism, although not a "philosophic religion" per se, for the most part does no violence to philosophy. Islam, particularly fundamental sects, gives no deference to philosophy, except for the mystical branches.

BUDDHISM - While the Buddhist theory of salvation differs in minor details from the Philosophic Atheism of the Ancient Greeks, its essential nature is the same. Therefore, the following will serve as an introduction into the salvation of both Buddhism and the Ancient Grecian Mysteries.

Buddhism considers deity only in the form of Self, or Absolute Existence, and has no concept of a personal God. Reincarnations occur within the lower spheres of the "Egg of Being"; those spheres being considered as the ground wherein is set up the wheel of necessity. Accordingly, pursuant to a great Buddhist philosopher, "Of births and deaths there are countless number, but one Great Death and one Great Birth is the measure of accomplishment."

Salvation to the Buddhist is reaching Nirvana. "Nirvana is reached when each finds himself to be all and rests forever in the state of Not-Being, which is All-Being, indivisible and perfect." "What keeps the soul bound in the cycle of birth, death, and re-birth? ~ desire and ignorance; of the two the greater evil is ignorance.

Lama Anagarika Govinda ("Creative Meditation and Multi-Dimensional Consciousness") writes:

> Therefore the Buddha silently held up a flower, when the pious pilgrim Subhadra wanted to know the quintessence of the Buddha's teaching. The flower, which opens itself to the light of heaven, while yet being rooted in the earth, belongs to the deepest symbols of the East. The darkness of the earth and the light of heaven; the powers of the depth, in which the experiences of an infinite past - of aeons of individual life forms - are stored, and the cosmic forces of the supra-individual, universal laws, are united in the blossom of spiritual enfoldment in conscious form.

HINDUISM - Hinduism, like Buddhism, is often called a philosophic religion. There are many different types of Hindu beliefs as there are significant differences in Christianity. The following is somewhat representative of Indian Wisdom.

The individuated soul was separated off from the Supreme soul. (In Christian terminology, this would be the Hindu "Fall of Man.") While still separated from the Supreme Soul, the individualized soul is "enclosed in a succession of cases (kosa), which envelope it and as it were, fold one over the other." The cases from innermost to outermost are: Ananda-maya-kosa, Vijnana-maya-kosa, Mano-maya, Pranamaya, and Anna-maya. One must climb through these cases in his cycle of birth and death until he reaches "The Hall of Vibhu, and the glory of Brahman reaches him." [Upanishad, I.2.]

Reaching the state of Brahman is the soul's final liberation from the lower nature and freedom from "samara", the wheel of cause and effect Salvation.

GNOSTICISM - Christian Mysticism and Gnosticism are of similar character and very philosophic in nature. Other than the Nag Hammadi Texts and the Dead Sea Scrolls, most of the common information extant regarding the Gnostics and their doctrines, stigmatized as heresy by the ante-Nicene Church Fathers, is derived from the writings of St. Irenaeus. The winner writes the history. Therefore, these types of commentaries must be viewed with caution, particularly, as in this case, the writer is an antagonist with an agenda.

Gnosticism was divided more or less into two major parts, commonly called the Syrian School and the Alexandrian School. These groups agreed on essentials, the latter division was more inclined to be pantheistic while the Syrian school was more dualistic. The Alexandrian School was the outgrowth of the teachings of Basilides, who claimed to have received his instruction directly from the Apostle Matthew. Gnostics, in the main, were emanationists and believed in a heaven and a hell. Salvation was derived through attunement rather than atonement.

JUDAISM - Salvation in Judaism is a somewhat nebulous concept. Jews believe in an afterlife and resurrection of the body; although resurrection of the body was not widely accepted until the Maccabian Period (c. 170 B.C.)

Pursuant to Gershom Scholem, the once popular concept of "Gilgul" or reincarnation lost favor in the Second Temple period. He points out however, that Josephus in "Antiquities" 18:1, 3 and in "Jewish Wars" 2:8, 14 writes that the Pharisees maintained their belief in Gilgul. Other Jewish scholars believe that one of the major divisions between the Pharisees and Sadducees was that the latter did not believe in reincarnation but the former did. It is interesting to note that the three greatest minds of Jewish history differ on Gilgul. Maimonides was silent on the subject; Rabbi Adam Plony rejects the idea; and the mystic Nahmanides embraced reincarnation and wrote extensively in support of the concept.

The Hebrews believe in a heaven and a hell. However, Jewish precepts and dogma concentrate mainly on this life and spend little time discussing the next. Instead of the widely held notion of "Be good or you will go to hell," the Jews believe they should keep God's commands because "He said to."

However, the mystical branch of Judaism, known as Kabbalahism is a true philosophic religion. Although most followers of Judaism do not embrace Kabbalahism, for the most part, they are not hostile to it.

ISLAM - Salvation in Islam comes from the acceptance of one's repentance and forgiveness of one's sins by the creator of all that exists. Salvation only comes from the guidance of God (Allah), there are no intercessors.

Salvation consists of three aspects:
1. Statement of the Tongue
2. Belief in the Heart (sincere intentions)
3. Action of the Limbs

All three aspects working in concert opens the door to salvation, and in essence substantiates faith. ~ There is no salvation without faith, and the omission of any one aspect nullifies one's opportunity for salvation. Removing a harmful object from a path, and modesty is part of faith.

The word "Muslim" translates as "one who submits." Muslims must submit to the following "Five Pillars of Islam": (1) believe that there is only one god and Muhammad is this prophet, (2) pray five times per day, (3) take care of the poor and needy, (4) participate in ritual fasts, and (5) make a pilgrimage to the holy city of Mecca.

"Jinnah" is paradise or heaven. One does not know in this life if he will enter Jinnah, it is only after death and the final judgment that his final destination is known.

Islam, as a rule, forbids free thinkers and tells its adherents what to do and how to think. In many parts of the world, any deviation is met with violence. This is in direct opposition to philosophy which by definition requires "free thinking." Sufism, the mystical branch of Islam, is much more philosophical in nature and to a degree tolerates, if not encourages, a certain amount of free thinking. Islamic fundamentalists do not view Sufi's as Muslims and have nothing but contempt for them and their beliefs.

By including theology/religion as one of the corners of his triangle, he was not referring to the "modern" religions that bar the philosophic thinker from practicing his craft. Rather, he was referring to religion as it was originally intended before its corruption by power hungry men.

Moses, the great Hebrew Philosopher, was raised in the House of Pharaoh and was trained in the philosophic mysteries of Egypt. The Egyptian Priests did not originate the truths contained in their teachings. The teachings were just a re-emphasis of an ever existing doctrine of truth. It is no well accepted; even by secular scholars that Moses did not "coin" a new religion, but simply repackaged and adapted the Mysteries of Isis to the needs of the Hebrew people. Over time, the Hebrews lost the spirit of the religion and became bogged down in the law.

The great Rabbi Jesus did not intend to start a new religion. He taught in the Synagogues using the same Hebrew Scriptures. He brought no new message, but ripped away the veil of dogma obscuring the innate truth of the Scriptures. It was those in power long after Jesus' death, who never actually knew him, that have once again placed a veil on the truth and chains on the masses.

Similarly, Muhammad, from his cave, did not pray for new truths, but for a way to restate and re-reveal the original truths in a manner that men in his environment may understand. It was those after his death that corrupted his teachings.

The philosophy of the ancients as recorded in the Mysteries is with us today, if we would but look. "Remove the sandals from your feet, for the place on which you are standing is holy ground." The first time most of us probably heard those words was in the reading of Exodus 3:5, where God called to Moses out of the burning bush. (This, according to the Scriptures, was Moses' initial communication from God, which started his Hebraic ministry; his initiation.) However, this was not the first time that Moses heard those words.

As mentioned earlier, Moses was raised in the Royal House as the son of Pharaoh's daughter. (Gen. 2:5-10) This necessarily meant that Moses was schooled in all exoteric and esoteric religious teachings. He would have also been initiated into the philosophic Mysteries of Isis. (See Plutarch, "Isis and Osiris," in Vol. V of the Moralia"; H. Frankfurt, "Ancient Egyptian Religion"; E.A. Wallis Budge, "The dwellers of the Nile")

The Greek Eleusinian, Bacchie and other philosophic Mystery Schools were based on the Egyptian Mysteries of Isis. (See To Taylor, "Imbilichus on the Mysteries.") Each of the Mystery Schools began the initiation process in the same manner. The initiate would enter the place of initiation by ascending a short stairs, usually seven steps (The same seven steps referred to earlier in the mysteries of Mithras) and entering a gate into the sanctuary. Immediately the Hierophant (Priet of the Mysteries) would state, "Remove the sandals from your feet, for the place on which you are standing is holy ground." (Id.)

In other words:

"He is required to put off common habits of earth that he may make ready for a new life. To understand adequately the meaning of this symbolical departure from the things that are behind him in his past to those that await him in the future is to take the first step towards knowledge ..." (A.E. Waite, "A New Encyclopedia." page 304.

The Ancient Philosophic Mysteries, known as the "Greater Mysteries" of the Greeks and the Foundational Mysteries of Ancient Egypt, were divided into Three (3) Degrees. The teaching of each successive degree became more and more in depth. The instruction in Higher Degrees did not invalidate that of the lower, but clarified, explained and expanded the wisdom.

This writer believes that the Bible is a text book guide to Invitation into the Greatest Mysteries of Jesus Christ. After a study of the Ancient Mysteries, It appears that the Holy Writ is patterned after those mysteries.

A. First eleven chapters of Genesis tell of the creation and fall ofman.

B .Genesis chapter twelve through Exodus Two relates the solidifying of our spiritual bondage to our lower selves (sin).

C. Exodus 3:5 is the entry into the Mysteries. "Remove the sandals from your feet"

D. Exodus four through the end of the Old Testament is the Firs Degree of the Mysteries.

E. Jesus' birth and ministry are the Second Degree of the Christian Mystery School.

F .Jesus' passion, death, resurrection and beyond tells of initiation into the Third and Final Degree of the Greatest Mysteries. It should be noted that the Final Degree begins with the "washing of the feet," which symbolism includes that of the sandals from Exodus 3:5.

G. The Book of Revelation is a veiled retelling of Initiation into the THREE Degrees of the Mysteries- thinly veiled to those familiar with the Greater Mysteries and oppressively obscure to those who have no clue of the Mysteries.

The above is the reason why one sees the Old Testament First Degree theology of God (wrathful, judgmental, smiting, and irrational) clarified, explained and expanded into the God of love in the Higher Degrees of the New Testament. Similarly, soul and after-life theology is primarily reserved for the Higher Degrees, which explains why the Hebrew Scriptures spent little time on this theology.

Let us increase the understanding of the Greater Mysteries of Jesus Christ as presented in the Three Degrees of Initiation of the Bible, this writer believes, may be greatly enhanced with an honest review of the Greater Greek Mysteries and Foundational Egyptian Mysteries.

Judaism, Christianity and Islam are all known as the religions of Abraham and all look to the Bible in varying degrees. It would be well for any judgmental adherents to these religions, who have contempt for the noble philosophy to study their respective religion's origin. Their eyes then may be opened to the truth that true religion is not in opposition to philosophy, but rather supports the discipline.

Philosophy always involves "God" in its system of thought, either as a starting point or an ending point. Before this can be explained we must first look at who or what is God. If someone asks, "Do you believe in God?" Most people in the United States would answer a resounding "Yes", and indeed in a recent Plow survey did just that. However, when asked that question, the philosopher, before answering, will say, Define God." As example, this writer does not believe in a wrathful god smiting entire races of people without reason and condemning countless billions of souls to a burning hell. (Many Christians believe that or 144,000 souls will be saved from "hell." (See Revelation 14:1) If that is the god the question is asking about, then no, this writer does not believe in that god. However, if the subject of the interrogation is the God of love, hope and mercy, then yes, that is the God that this writer believes in and embraces.

Whether we start with God or end with God in our philosophy search depends greatly on our concept of deity. The seeker may attribute various qualities and attributes to God and then, using that as the stating point, contemplate and seek the necessary processes and conditions that created the visible physical universe. Or one may start with the emotional universe and believing that the observable physical was created by divine movement, through contemplation seek to understand qualities of the deity capable of creating such vastness.

The ancient philosopher believed in deity and proceeded to contemplate the construction of the universe. The modernist, obscured by science and technology, sees the vastness of the universe and then looks for God. However, the mind trained in the last few centuries is thought of the supremacy of science, and as God can not be seen by science, may eliminate God from the original equation entirely. Or he may ascribe such a week and impotent God (because of his inability to see God with his telescopes and experiments) that God becomes a "non-entity" and at best a footnote to the individual. This latter individual is identified in Laplace, the great astronomer of the late 17th and early 18th century. After reading his great work on astronomy, Napoleon stated, "But you make no mention of God," which elicited the great science reply, "Sire, I have no need for that hypothesis." However, just because one may have a great scientific mind does not mean that his philosophic senses have been dulled. One of the greatest scientists of all time, Albert Einstein remained a firm believer in God. In fact, he stated that the more he learned through his scientific endeavors, the greater and deeper the awe he had for God.

Pythagoras said that once the triangle is determined, any problem is two-thirds solved. We are triune beings with a body, soul and spirit. All life is triangular; all existence is triangular. Life is divine, and eternal; matter is fleeting and impermanent. The building agent is the full measure of being. The great philosophic mystery schools of ancient times that the spirit was the divine

substance, the part worked upon was the physical matter, and that the spirit was so far superior to the physical that there needed to be a binding and animating agent as a mediatory between the two. Certain of these philosophic schools taught that there were "eighty thousand degrees of intelligence" intervening between the elemental and the eternal. (It is interesting to note that in Tibetan Buddhism, there are eighty thousand gods performing various functions.)

Philosophy tells us that the "Law of Sympathy" requires that the "intervening intelligence" must have a measure of the consciousness of both the higher and the lower. The followers of the teachings of Pythagoras know as Pythatoreans allegorically supported this premise when they would say, "there are three kinds of creatures: gods, men, and Pythagoras." The great philosopher represents the mediating intelligence between higher and lower. It is only through philosophy that one can truly even begin to know the relationships between the greater and the less.

Sages throughout time have referred to the state of man unenlightened by philosophy as being asleep. The ancients would teach that most men are walking around asleep, spending all of their time, energy, wealth and thought on trinket, matter, the lowest form. It is interesting to note that in the holy writ it states that a great sleep came upon Adam (man), but it never states that he woke up. (Gen 2:21) If man is ever to rise from the state of a brute, he must awaken to the glory of the higher. It has been the philosopher who has, throughout the ages, taken the vanguard for humanity and raised the banner of mindfulness. This is the gift of philosophy, the true meaning of the discipline, to awaken the individual and open all mankind to awareness.

FIVE GREAT PHILOSOPHERS PHILOSOPHORUM QUENTUM MAGUM

History is replete with great thinkers that have helped shape society and made us what we are. These have been numerous odes, songs, poems and legends of these extraordinary men and women. Even the most base and mundane mind will often recognize names like the Greek Socrates, Plato and Aristotle; the Chinese Lao Tzu and Confucius; the Indian Prince Siddhartha Guatama, commonly known as "The Buddha", as well as the Persian Zoroastor; and even the Hebrew Enoch, Moses and Jesus. However, few understand the awesome contribution these philosophers have made. Even fewer have heard of other men of no ordinary intellect and the immensity of the contribution to society like Francis Bacon, Elias Ashmole and Philippus Aureolus Theophrastus Bombastus von Hohenheim, perhaps better known as Paracelsus.

I will attempt to do justice to five great men of philosophy. Instead of selecting philosophers who carry the most recognizable names, I have chosen five who have had the greatest impact on my life. Those who have directly influenced my way of thinking, my actions and feelings. The men discussed below are no less great than Confucius, The Buddha or Enoch, though some are not as well recognized. These men, their teachings and their lives are important not just to me, but to all who walk, whether awakened or not. I will start with two recognized names, Pythagoras and Plato.

PYTHAGORAS

The Oracle of Delphi was one of the greatest wonders of antiquity. It operated for a millennium and a half and was the richest of the ancient temples. People would travel from all over the, "known world", seeking information about the future or anything of concern. The sheer number of adherents to the temple attests to belief in the accuracy of that given in response.

In the Sixth Century B.C., as the legend reveals, Mnesarchus and his wife Parthenis, decided to consult the Oracle of Delphi concerning business. Rather than answering that which was sought, when the Prophetess of Apollo Pythoness spoke in her hexameter verse, Mnesarchus and Parthenis were shocked to hear, through the five Hosii, or Holy Men, interpreting the utterances, that Parthenis was pregnant. This child, as the prophecy continued, would grow to "surpass all men in beauty and wisdom, and who throughout the course of his life would continue much to the benefit of mankind." Pythagora, as the circle said, was born at Sidon in Phoenicia. Bolstered by the prophecy, the merchant Mnesarchus spared no expense in the education and training of the young Pythagorces.

> "After having acquired all which was possible for him to learn of the Greek Philosophers and, presumably, become initiate in the Eleusinian Mysteries, he went to Egypt, and after many rebuffs and refusals, finally succeeded in securing initiation in the Mysteries of Isis, at the hands of the priests of Thebes. Then this intrepid 'joiner' wended his way into Phoenicia and Syria where the Mysteries of Adonis were conferred upon him, and crossing to the Valley of the Euphrates he tarried long enough to become versed in the secret lore of the Chaldeans, who still dwelt in the vicinity of Babylon. Finally, he made his greatest and most historic venture through media and Persia into Hindustan where he remained several years as a pupil and initiate of the learned Brakmins of Elephenta and Ellort.

(See Ancient Freemasonry, by Frank C. Higgins, 32")

Some estimate that Pythagoras was initiated into as many as fourteen different secret societies. After his travels, he settled in the Doria colony of Crotona in Southern Italy. He opened a school of devoted disciples. He taught those that followed him the secrets of mathematics, music and astronomy, which he considered the Triad of "The Great Sciences."

Any high school sophomore in America taking basic geometry will learn of the Pythagorean Theorem, which is $A2 + B2 = C2$ relating to any right triangle, or, the sum of the square of the sides equals the hypotenuse squared. This is the extent of most people's knowledge of this great Philosopher. A precious few know that Pythagoras taught that this theorem was one of the great occult fundamentals in the creation of the material universe and relationship of 3-4-5 [(3x3) + (4x4) = (5x5)] was the exact proportions of mercury, salt and sulfur need to accomplish the Philosopher's Stone of Alchemy.

Most of what we know of the teachings of Pythagoras comes from Thomas Taylor's translation of the "Life of Pythagoras" written by Iamblichus, which Taylor first published in London in 1818. According to Iamblichus, one of the great Philosophers favorite statements was:

> "We must avoid with our utmost endeavor, and amputate with fire and sword, and by all means, from the body, sickness; from the soul, ignorance; from the belly, luxury; from the city, sedition; from the family, discord; and from all things, excess."

The students in his school in Crotona were divided into two categories called "Exoterici", which were those given the secret wisdom. (Higgins, Ancient Freemasonry") Out of this last group, Iamblichus lists 218 and 17 women among the most famous and influential of the Philosopher's students.

Pythagoras married one of his disciples when he was sixty years old, and the couple had seven children.

"In height he exceeded six feet; his body was perfectly formed as that of Apollo. Pythagoras was the personification of majesty and power, and in his presence all felt humble and afraid. As he grew older, his physical powers increased rather than waned, so that as he approached the century mark he was actually in the prime of life." (I.D.)

He was outspoken and very critical of those in power. His unyielding censure of the level politicos led to his and his school's destruction. Spurred (and probably hired) by local officials, a

band of thugs burned the school and killed one of the greatest men to have ever walked the earth.

Yet, they could not kill the wisdom that lies and blesses us even today.

PLATO

Plato believed the highest and greatest good the Creator had bestowed upon man was Philosophy. Many however, believe that the greatest blessing was Plato.

It is estimated that Plato was born about 427 B.C. and died some 74 years later. Arguably, the greatest teacher of all times was Socrates. It was the Master Socrates who took Plato under his wings and imparted his wisdom upon Plato. In addition to his training with Socrates, Plato traveled extensively and, much like Pythagoras, studied in various Mystery Schools.

> "Plato was initiated into the 'Greater Mysteries' at the age of 49. The initiation took place in one of the subterranean halls of the Great Pyramid in Egypt. The Isiac Table formed the alter, before which the Divine Plato stood and received that which was always his, but which the ceremony of the Mysteries enkindled and brought from its dormant state. With this ascent, after three days in the Great Hall, he was received by the Hierophant of the Pyramid (the Hierophant was seen only by those who had passed the three days, the three degrees, the three dimensions) and given verbally the Highest Esoteric Teachings, each accompanied with Its appropriate Symbol. After a further three month's sojourn in the halls of the Pyramid, the Initiate Plato was sent out into the world to do the work of the Great Order, as Pythagoras and Orpheus had been before him."

(See Thomas Taylor, Six Books of Prochus on the Theology of Plato, London, 1816)

Upon his return from Egypt, Plato formed a group of thinkers into an academy known as the Academic Philosophers. Cicero states that in this school, Plato would teach three main areas of Philosophy: ethics, physics, and dialectics. Ethics as considered by Plato was the science of character, morality and individual responsibility, and dealt with the nature of good. Physics included the observation and contemplation of the observable. Plato's greatest student, Aristotle, carried Plato's physics to greater lengths, which he called metaphysics. Dialectics is derived from the Greek word meaning "to conserve." It was used differently by different Philosophers. Socrates' question and answer technique of teaching was called dialectics, whereas to Plato it meant the study of forms.

Plato taught that there were three orders of being: the unmoved mover, the self-moved, and that which is moved. He stated that "the one" is the best term to describe God or the Absolute. The one is the whole and precedes division and diversity

"Let none ignorant of geometry enter here", was written above the entrance to his academy. He continually reminded his students that his greatest disciple was Aristotle (384-322 B.C.). In fact, if Aristotle was not at one of his classes, he would say, "The intellect is not here." He would also refer to Aristotle as, "The mind of the school."

After Plato's death in about 347 B.C., his students split into two groups. The "Academics" stayed at the academy he started, and the "Peripatetics" headed by Aristotle, moved to Lyceum.

FRANCIS BACON

Sir Francis Bacon, after much contemplation of the external things observed, along with several others, is credited with founding the systems of modern science and philosophy. Lord Bacon was born the son of Queen Elizabeth and the Earl of Leicester in 1561 and he was reported to have died in 1626. However, it is doubtful that his funeral and resulting obituary were factual. Bacon lived in a time when free thinkers in general and a great philosopher in particular, would be considered a major threat to the Church and Crown alike. The Church was even quicker to burn someone at the stake for heresy than the State would take someone's head for sedition.

It has been well established that Bacon was chosen by the King to review the manuscript of the King James Bible "it will eventually be proved that the whole scheme of the Authorized Version of the Bible was Francis Bacon's." (See William T. Smedley's, The Mystery of Francis Bacon.)

The most cursory review by even the philosophic neophyte of the plays and sonnets of the Band of Avon will yield a treasure trove of philosophic truths. Indeed, the works of William Shakespeare have been viewed as some of the great philosophic writing of all time. There have been volumes written supporting that the actor Shakespeare would have been unable to complete the writings attributed to him. These books give significant; if not compelling evidence that the true author of the plays and sonnets was in fact, Sir Francis Bacon.

A few of these arguments are summarized as follows:

William Shakespeare was schooled in the town of Stratford, born to illiterate parents, and had a distain for learning. Bacon was highly educated.

An extensive library would be needed as reference material to write with authority works placed in various ages. Shakespeare did not possess even a meager library, whereas Bacon owned thousands of volumes.

The author of the works was required to have secure knowledge of French, Italian, Spanish, Danish, Latin, and Greek. Ben Johnson, an intimate friend of Shakespeare said he knew "small Latin and less Greek." Bacon was fluent in all but a few of those languages.

The high philosophic ideals interspersed throughout all the works required that the author was familiar with the great philosophers. There is no record of Shakespeare having education or knowledge of philosophy; Bacon however was a Platonist, a Qabbalist and a Pythagorean.

(See W.F.C. Wigston, "Francis Bacon Versus Phantom Captian Shakespeare, London 1981).

The above items scarcely scratch the surface of the evidence supporting the case for Bacon.

Once the plays and sonnets are viewed as great philosophical works by one of the greatest philosophers of all time, the words become illuminated with truth and learning; a melodic university of the highest order.

After Sir Bacon's mock funeral in 1626, he was reported to have moved to Germany and formed a secret philosophical society. Many of the writings of Bacon were printed on paper bearing the watermarks of the Rosicrucian or Masonic Orders.

It has been said that the unknown history and lost rituals of Freemasonry and of the Rosiccrucians may be rediscovered in the symbolism and cryptograms of the writings of Bacon. Though Christianity did great violence and destruction to the greater mysteries of Egypt and Greece, through Bacon the philosophic truth are still available to the most ardent student.

ELIAS ASHMQLE

The son of a saddler and grandson of a draper, Elias Ashmole was born in 1617. He learned early that he did not want to be a laborer or tradesman but would rather study philosophy. "That I might be able to live to myself and studies, without being forced to take pains for a livelihood in the world." In 1638 he moved to his boyhood home to practice law. He was an ardent supporter of the king, and had a voracious need for women and money.

In pursuit of his needs he moved to Oxford where he divorced his first wife, married his second wife, who was a very wealthy relative of his first wife. He enjoyed the being free from employment and having the funds to continue his studies and even collect a substantial number of philosophic works, some very rare. However, his marriage was constantly in turmoil due to his wife's relatives. They continually filed over 800 pages of pleadings seeking a divorce and freezing him out of her wealth. The court ruled in Ashmole's favor, denied his wife's petition for divorce and determined he was entitled to his wealth.

On October 16, 1646, pursuant to his diary, he "was made a Freemason at Warrington in Lancashire." Five years later he compiled what is arguably the greatest work in the English language regarding the Alchemical pursuits of the philosopher's stone. His work, "Theatrum Chemicum Britannicum," includes several practical treatises from great English Philosophers, with annotations by Ashmole.

Using the works as a cornerstone of study, the door to the extraordinary world of the Divine Mysteries of hermetic philosophy is opened. Ashmole made it clear that the highest and best branch of hermetic philosophy is the transmutation of the soul of the philosopher.

> As this is but a part so it is the least share of that blessing which may be acquired by the Philosopher's Materia, if the full virtue thereof were known. Gold, I confess is a delicious object, a goodly light which we admire and gaze upon ut pueri in Junonis avem; but to make gold is the chief intent of the Alchemist, so was it scarcely an intent of the ancient Philosophers and the lowest use the Adepti made of this Materia. For they, being lovers of wisdom more than worldly wealth, drove at higher and more excellent operations; and certainly he to whom the whole course of Nature lies open rejoiceth not so much that he can make gold and silver or the devils be made subject to him as that he sees the heavens open, the angels of God ascending and descending and that his own name is fairly written in the Book of Life.

(Ashmole, "Theatrum Chemicum Britannicum)

The works of Ashmole help the philosopher to keep his endevors in proper perspective. The true goal of the philosopher should not be to gain knowledge for knowledge's sake, but for a complete transformation on the soul level.

PARACELSUS

Francis Barrett, in his "Biographia Antiqua," describes Pracelsus as,

> "The Prince of Physicians and Philosophers of Fire; Grand Paradoxical Physician; the Ttrismegistus of Switzerland; First Reformer of Chymical Philosophy; Adept in Alchemy; Cabala and Magic; Nature's Faithful Secretary; Master of the Elixir of Life and the Philosopher's Stone, and the Great Monarch of Chymical Secrets.

Born on December 17, 1493, under the name Philippus Aureolus Theophrastus Bombastus von Hohenheim, Pracelsus was the greatest philosopher to come out of Switzerland. Both of his parents worked in healthcare, his father a physician and his mother in charge of a hospital. He was an only child and vowed that he would reform medical practices.

At the age of twenty, he began a twelve year trek through various countries of Europe, Asia, India and parts of Africa seeking to learn from the great philosophers of his day. After his travels he settled in Germany and began to apply the great wisdom he gained in science, religion and philosophy. He immediately incurred wrath of the established medical community because of his radical ideas. Undeterred, he boldly proclaimed that "some day all doctors of Europe would turn from the other school and, follow him, revere him above every other physician."

Such statements hardly enamored him with the local medical community. Lt. Col. Fielding Garrisom, M.D., in his celebrated "Introduction to the History of Medicine," described Paraclesus as "the precursor of chemical pharmacology and therapeutics, and the most original medical thinker of the 16th century." As rejected as he was by the medical aristocracy of his day, he was embraced by the philosophic community. He influenced great thinkers like Fludd and Lessing, and was known in his time as the "Swiss Hermes." His writings and those of others like Robert Turner, Stephen Trigge, and Raymond Lully impact the philosophic mind today.

His medical cures were remarkable and often called miracles. This enraged his enemies even more. He was called a "vagabond filled with wanderlust" and condemned for his efforts to reconcile medicine with the philosophy and religions. Paraclesus was not afraid to seek knowledge from any class of society or from any location no matter how remote. Of this he wrote,

> Therefore I consider that it is for me a matter of praise, not of blame, that I have hitherto and worthily pursued my wanderings. For this will I bear witness respecting nature: he who will investigate her ways must travel her brooks with his feet. That which is written is investigated through it's letters, but nature from land to land - as often a land so often a leaf. Thus is the codex of nature, thus must it's leaves be turned.

(See John Maxon Stillman's, "Paracelsus")

Paracelsus tried to educate the masses in philosophy, medicine, and life. He was the first to write scientific books in the language of the common people, His primary Hypothesis was that everything created was good for something and that all things had a spiritual component. He adamantly encouraged everyone to investigate the profundity of nature, science, religion and philosophy.

The aforementioned five men of genius each expound the great value of philosophy and that the highest wisdom is the application of the philosophic knowledge gained. If philosophy is study for knowledge's sake, it will be of little more value than studying and memorizing all the individual stats of the New York Giants. It should be the goal of all humankind to grow and transform. Both the neophyte seeker and the most advanced adept would do well to read and study these five eminent Philosophers who have such a tremendous impact on my life.

ETHICS DEFINED

Ethics is the study and implementation of goodness and the standard of right and wrong. It has been referred to as moral philosophy and the theory of choices.

Ethics, on the macro-level deals with war and peace, abortion, euthanasia, the death penalty, and the value of all life, human and animal. On the micro-level it deals with everyday decisions, both small and great, of each individual. Should I cheat on my taxes? Or should I cheat on my wife? Should I donate money or time to help the poor? Should I seek virtue and the good of others or selfishness and instant gratification? These questions can only be answered by the individual based on his standard of ethics.

THE ESSENCE OF ETHICS

It is easy to define ethics as the study of the standards of conduct and moral judgment. But I believe that it is far more than that prosaic definition. To me, ethics is the most personal of all disciplines within philosophy. Ethics is the conduct we use to answer some of the most important questions in our lives: "What should I do?", "How should I live?" "What are my goals in life?" "Am I my brother's keeper?" Etc.

In the Holy Writ, the ancient penman wrote, "I have set before you today life and prosperity, death and adversity. *** Choose this day whom you will serve." This is the essence of ethics. Each moment there is a decision before us; how we decide is based on ethics.

In earlier times ethics was not synonymous with morality, but rather a branch of inquiry that studies morality. However, in modern times the terms morality and ethics have become interchangeable.

The ancient philosophers would teach that virtue is the crowning element of truth; without virtue there can be no pureness of the heart, of the soul and of the mind, and that true understanding only comes through virtue. The foundation of virtue is ethics. Without making the correct choices there is no virtue; without ethics there is no basis upon which to make the right decisions. It is only through ethics that we may be invested with the inner wisdom and power to do what is right and noble and just.

The link between ethics, morality, virtue, understanding, and true happiness are so firmly forged it is impossible to have one without the others. Each of these are inextricably intertwined, with the first step being ethics. The easiest path is not always the best route; instant gratification usually leads to pain and suffering. It is ethics that allows us to stand tall, forsake the easy for the just, and deny ourselves immediate pleasure for the greater good of ourselves and others.

KING SOLOMON

The name Solomon may be divided into three syllables, SOL - OM -ON, symbolizing light, glory, and truth collectively and respectively

***

Solomon, the Spirit of Universal Illumination - mental, spiritual, moral, and physical - is personified in the king of an earthly nation.

(Manly P. Hall, "The Secret Teachings of All Ages," pages 175 to 176)

Solomon was the third king of Israel (c. 961 - 922 B.C.), and the son of King David and Bathsheba, the product of an adulterous relationship (Bathsheba was the wife of Uriah the Hittite, a ranking member of David's army). He died in c. 922 B.C.

Most of what we know about Solomon and his reign comes from the Hebrew Bible, known as the Old Testament in Christendom and writings of Freemasons. The Masonic writings are mostly allegorical in nature and will not be discussed here

Solomon was known for his ethics and wisdom. Flavious Josephus, in his "Eighth Book of the Antiquities of the Jews," wrote, "Now the sagacity and wisdom which God had bestowed on Solomon was so great that he exceeded the ancients, in so much that he was in no way inferior to the Egyptians, who are said to have been beyond all men in understanding."

The most celebrated action by Solomon involving ethics, morality and wisdom is found in 1 Kings 3:16-28. In this case, two prostitutes came to the king for him to decide who should keep the baby in question. (Both prostitutes had babies, but one died at night and there was a dispute as to who the child's mother was.) After pleading their case, Solomon said to cut the baby in two and each get half. He said this knowing that the true mother of the child would give up her baby before allowing him to be killed. Solomon was right; the true mother said, "No, don't kill him. Give it to

her!" The non-mother said, "Cut it in two." The king then knew who the real mother was and awarded her the child.

Solomon's early reign was replete with instances of ethical and wise decisions. He sought peace and made alliances with Egypt and Phoenicia. Even though Hiram, king of Tyre offered Solomon free supplies and labor to build the temple, he instead paid him a price that was more than fair.

Later in his reign he dropped his ethical guard and started womanizing and heavily taxed the tribes of Israel, which brought a revolt after his death.

His ethics and wisdom lives on in the writings attributed to him, the Song of Solomon, the Deuterocanonical Wisdom of Solomon, and most significantly Proverbs.

PRINCIPLES DEFINED

A principle is a foundational law, a fundamental truth upon which others are based. To find the principle, one must first wash away the mundane. However, before even the falsity may be cleansed away to reveal the truth, one must have been awakened enough to understand the false from the true.

As example, everyone has thoughts and options, most are based on emotional rather than principle. The "law of thought", known as the principle of non-contradiction dating back to the peripatetic school of Aristotle, has two parts: A statement cannot be both true and false; nothing can have a quality like green, and not have it at the same time.

PRENTIUM PRINCIPUM
(The Value Of Principles)

The proof that the universe has been established by principle (law) is all around us if we would but look. If we eat too much, the principles governing the assimilation of food renders us fat. The principles of attraction, motion and force keep the stars in the heavens and allow the earth to sustain life. We can spend our lives asleep groveling for trinkets until we die, or we can awaken to the truth of all things, seek the principle in all and live in harmony with that principle. Persistence and virtue may even lead to the ultimate, identification and oneness with the Principle of Principles, that which religion calls God.

Two thousand years ago a sect of pious Hebrew mystics lived near Mt. Carmel in the region of the Dead Sea, also known by the modern day Arabic term Qumran. The members of this Syrian sect were known as the Essenes. The etymology of the name "Essenes" is not definitively known, but most scholars believe it relates to some form of "physician" or "healer." Great miracles have been ascribed to this sect similar to those attributed to the philosophic Master Jesus. The great Jewish historian Josephus wrote about them in the most noble of terms, "they teach the immortality of the soul and esteem that the rewards of righteousness are to be earnestly striven for." The Essenes attributed their "abilities" to virtue together with the knowledge and understanding of principles. The rituals and practices of the group were extensive and demanding of discipline. Their "main" practice dealt with what they termed as the "Three Holy Streams of Life," or the "Three Principles of the Angels." The angelology of the Essenes was perhaps the most extensive of all ancient sects.

The Three Holy Streams included, "The Holy Stream of Life," "The Holy Stream of Sound" and "The Holy Stream of Light." Before one of their followers could attempt unity with the principles of life, sound and light, they first needed to master the seven principles of man.

The preamble to each practice dealing with the three principles of the angels was memorized, and recited aloud with internal knowing, it reads:

Into the inner most circle have you come, into the Mystery of Mysteries, that which was old when our Father Enoch was young and walked the Earth. Around and around have you come on your journey of many years always following the Path of Righteousness and living according to the Holy Law and Sacred Vows of our Brotherhood. Many years have you shared the daylight hours with the Angels of the Earthly Mother; many nights have you slept in the arms of the Heavenly Father taught by his unknown Angels. You have learned that the Principles of the Son of Man are seven of the Angels three and of God one. You shall now know of the three Principles of the Angels, The Mystery the Three Holy Streams, and the ancient way to traverse them. So shall you bathe in the light of Heaven, and at last behold the Principle of Principles, the Law of God which is One.

("The Essene Gospel Of Peace", Edmond Bordeaux Szekely)

Although the Essenes considered themselves Jewish, their practices were philosophic in nature. The conflict we see between religion and philosophy was not always so. In fact Pythagoras, perhaps the greatest of all philosophers, and the Master who coined the word "philosopher," taught that religion and science together with philosophy comprised the Pythagorean Theory of Triads, second only to the triad of the Monad, or God.

Whenever any system of government or religion deviates from its principle of helping its people and seeks to limit and control them, it becomes corrupted; it has been said that power corrupts and absolute power corrupts absolutely. Although this was said in relation to government, it is no less true for religion. The suppression of the mind and the masses by organized religion is

even more insidious than by government; government suppresses openly, while religion harms under the guise of altruism.

When the Master Jesus walked the earth, he called the pharisaic and sadducic tyrants "a brood of vipers." The Apostle Paul, in keeping with this theme stated that "the letter killeth, but the spirit gives life." In modern times we call these fundamental religious tyrants the pejorative term, "Bible Thumper." These are the individuals that attempt to suppress the free thinkers from pursuing philosophic principles by holding their Bibles high in the air, tapping them with their index finger as an apparent sign of authority and demanding that all think like them-that all read the Holy Writ not just literally, but "their" literal interpretation. They will stand tall and decree, "There is no deeper meaning! There is no true philosophy! All is folly except what I teach!" One of the greatest tragedies of the advent of the Bible Thumper is the sheer number of people following them.

The literalists do violence to the profundity of Sacred Scriptures; they turn the words into fetishes and idols; to these narrow thinkers, symbolism is unsearchable and therefore, in their mind, incapable of revealing greater truths. They is unable to see beyond the impermanent vehicle of the principle and onto the abstract reality of the principle itself.

Moses Maimonides, the most learned of the Rabbins and philosopher of the twelfth century, perhaps the greatest Jewish philosopher, devoted his life to the study and contemplation of the true meaning of the Hebrew Scriptures. Relating to the hidden meanings and true principles of the book of Genesis, Maimonides writes:

> We should not take literally that which is written in the Book of Creation nor entertain the same concepts of it as are common with the vulgar. If it were otherwise, our learned ancient sages would not have taken so much pains to conceal the sense, and to keep before the eyes of the uninstructed the veil of allegory which conceals the truths which it contains. Taken literally, the work contains the most extravagant and absurd idea of the Deity. Whoever can guess at the true meaning should take care not to divulge it. This is a maxim inculcated by our own wise men, especially in connection with the work of the six days. It is possible that by our own intelligence, or by the aid of others, some may guess the true meaning, in which case they should be silent respecting it; or, if they do speak of it, they should do so obscurely, as I myself do, leaving the rest to be guessed at by those who have sufficient ability to understand me.

It was an absolute practice in the mystery schools that the initiate had to take a vow of silence, which demanded death if the secrets be revealed.

Pursuant to Thomas Taylor, "Plato was initiated into the 'Greater Mysteries' at the age of 49. The initiation took place in one of the subterranean halls of the Great Pyramid of Egypt." Alexander Wilder in his "Philosophy and Ethic of Zoroaster," published in 1885, stated that Plato was severely criticized for revealing too many of the secret philosophic principles of the Mysteries to the general public in his writings.

The philosophic principles of the Greater Mysteries have had a substantial impact on civilization and are still having a significant positive impact today. In his "General History Of Freemasonry," Robert Macoy, 33° states, "It appears that all the perfection of civilization, and all the advancement made in philosophy, science and are among the ancients are due to those institutions which under the veil of mystery, sought to illustrate the most sublime truths of religion, morality, and virtue, and impress them on the hearts of their disciples. - Their chief object was to teach the doctrine of one God, the resurrection of man to eternal life, the dignity of the human soul, and to lead the people to see the shadow of the deity, in beauty, magnificence, and splendor of the universe."

The philosophic mystery schools would teach that there is a tremendous difference between knowledge, understanding and wisdom. To the initiate, all three should be sought with zeal, but knowledge without more was sin. Knowledge is just an accumulation of facts. Most anyone today, can find information on any subject on the internet. That information can be assimilated by the individual, but that does not mean he understands what he just read. Even if the information is understood it does no good to anyone unless that knowledge and understanding is acted upon. Wisdom was defined as the moving force of understanding. The vulgar go through life asleep or half-asleep not even knowing what a principle is. They just see the outward manifestation of a principle and believe that is the all. Even if they stumble upon a principle they do not understand it, much less being able to consciously walk within principle.

The mystery schools spent no little effort in instituting systems of observation and definite discipline which would teach the initiate how to strip away the mundane and seek the principle behind that contemplated.

The rituals of the ancient mysteries are scorned by modern man - religious and secular. We have become a society of instant gratification. Our attention span has been contracted to the length of time between commercials on television. We need excitement in our leisure time; sex and violence are the norm. In short we have become a society of the five senses. Rachel Ray's cooking show is one of the most popular in day time television. We need good food; many live for good food. Most labor for trinkets, leisure time fun and delicious food. Very few even care about principles and fewer still would know what a principle is, even if it bit them on the intellect. We are more in need of the teachings and rituals of the philosophic mysteries than ever.

Modern science and technology is good and very good, but when society looks to science for salvation, technology becomes a fetish and man is no more foolish than the primitives of prehistory. In the United States we put our trust in our great military might, never realizing that all warrior societies are destined to failure. How can any society succeed that seeks the superficial and has no clue of the profundity of principles?

The same question could have been asked in any era at any time. The truth, in the past and here today, is that in each age there was always those heroes of mankind who embraced principles and the philosophy that leads them there. To the superior intellect, ritualism is seen as an integral part of realization, not the empty ritual of zombie-like parishioners who have no clue of what the ritual represents, but only going through the motions. Those precious few of each era who have venerated the great philosophic thinkers and rituals of the greater mysteries are the saviors of society. There has never been a time when society digressed beyond the point of saving. We may not know today who these heroes will be that will reawaken the fire within and lead us back to the rituals of the mysteries, but they are among us.

The ceremonies of the Mysteries were formulated by the sages of old to reveal to the inner perceptions the principles of universal order. It is hard for the modern man to conceive of being able to walk the earth with the Divine. The Mysteries and the root of all true religions were based on the fundamental principle of right thinking, right feeling and right action leading to right knowing. Therefore, the principle of right knowing can only come through virtue or what the religious community calls righteousness. It is interesting to note that the Eightfold Path to Enlightenment in Buddhism is basically the same as the philosophic principle of right thinking, right feeling and right action leading to right knowing: 1) right view, 2) right aspiration, 3) right speech, 4) right action, 5) right livelihood, 6) right effort, 7) right mindfulness, and 8) right concentration.

It is not surprising that Buddhism is the closest of today's major religions to the schools of philosophic principles of the ancient Greeks. In their essence, enlightenment to the Buddhist, right knowing to the philosopher and salvation to the other major religions are all the same.

To the modern religious, "faith" is the be all and end all, rather then the principle of "right knowing." The Greater Mysteries of the Greeks, which in large measure were patterned after the Egyptian Mysteries, viewed faith as a "good start" for the neophyte, but was considered far inferior to the principle of right knowing. (See Plutrach, "Isis and Osiris," in vol. V of the "Moralia"; H.

Frankfurt, "Ancient Egyptian Religion", E.A. Wallis Budge, "The Dwellers of the Nile; T.Taylor, "Iamilichus on the Mysteries.")

The ancients would teach, as does the Holy Writ that "faith" comes through the five senses -from outside to within; "faith comes by hearing." This concept of gaining knowledge and faith from without is nothing more than a repackaging of religion by observation practiced by the most primitive cave dwellers.

Most modernists, blinded by their gods of science are quick to say that none can know God because God can not be proven to exist by their science. The true philosopher however, knows that the greatest measure of knowledge of the Principle of Principles or God does not and cannot come from without, but can only come from within. In ancient philosophy, as well as Christianity, man is a triune being. This principle of the triad is written in the New Testament, "May the God of peace himself sanctify you entirely - and may your <u>spirit</u> and <u>soul</u> and <u>body</u> be kept sound ..." (I Thes 5:23)

The soul may be destroyed, but not the spirit, for the spirit is that individualized portion of God within us. It is the spirit that beckons us to the higher. (See Matt 10:28; 16:26; Mk 8:36; Acts 2:27-31; James 1:21; 5:20; I Pet 1:9; 1:22; 2:11; 3 John2)

Indeed, the word of God is living and active, sharper than any two-edged sword, piercing until it divides soul from spirit... Heb. 4:12:

> The highest of all selves, the ultimate self of the universe, is God. The New Testament speaks of man as body, soul and spirit. The body
>
> is the thought-form through which the individuality finds expression on our present limited plane; the soul is a man's consciousness of himself as apart from all the rest of existence, and even from God; the spirit is the true being thus limited and expressed, - it is the deathless divine within us. The soul, therefore, is what we make it; the spirit we can neither make nor mar, for it is at once our being and God's.

(R.J. Campbell, "The New Theology," page 34.)

"These, then, are the major elements in the constitution of man: (1) The spirit, which is the eternal foundation and the abiding reality, by virtue of which man is immortal, superior to both beginnings and ends, and eternal in his own heavenly nature; (2) The soul, which is the intermediary by which the life in each ... manifests through vices and virtues; (3) The body, which being of earth earthly, is the framework wherein the higher nature ... " M.P. Hall, "Lectures on Ancient Philosophy," page 391.

"Thus the supreme world outside of man exists within man as the environment of his divine spirit (spirit), the superior world in the environment of the soul spirit (soul), and the inferior world in the environment of the body spirit (body)" Id., page 387.

The Greater Mysteries as well as religion teaches that that portion of the "individual" that is affected by the lower (sin and selfishness), is the soul and through disease, the body. The spirit cannot be affected by our wrongdoing. Sin was always a function of selfishness and selfishness the result of a belief in duality. If the actor understands the principal of unity or one, he then knows that any violence done to another is actually violence done to oneself; this self-abuse is done to the soul.

The ancients would teach the great principle that likes attract. It is through faith that one may have virtue, (right thinking, right feeling, and right action). It is then this virtue that aligns the soul with the breath of God within known as the spirit. In Judeo-Christian terminology, the Holy Spirit of God is always beckoning to our spirit to aid us in moving higher. However, we, our

individuality and personality which comprise the soul, of which our conscious minds are a part, cannot recognize the higher calling and information available through the spirit unless we have resonance with the higher through the principle of attunement. It is through this principle that we can have a higher knowing that is unavailable from without. The Mysteries teach that true understanding (knowing) is beyond the reason of the senses. Faith comes through the senses; hence, true knowing cannot come through faith. True understanding is:

> The power to experience and interpret the laws (or principles) that govern the expression of Creative Force (the Principles of Principles), or God, in and through the physical, mental and spiritual bodies of humanity. Where there is virtue there will be understanding, for one follows the other. Understanding is the reward of virtue [right thinking, right feeling and right action]. With virtue, therefore, comes understanding, for the two are as the tenon and the mortise; they fit one with the other.

("A Search For God," A.R.E. Press)

Therefore, faith is itself, a principle that we can use to allow us to approach the Principle of Principles.

As far as the modern religious have corrupted the principle of faith, it is not surprising that these same individuals have corrupted the principle of prayer. Prayer today is used by many to beg and curry favor with an all powerful white-haired man sitting on a throne in the sky for favors. The principal of prayer was not always so.

> I open towards light and lift myself to God on the perfume of prayer. I ask for nothing beyond myself. I own everything I need. I am content in the company of God, a prayer that contains its own answer. I am the lotus. As if from a dream, I wake up laughing.

(Papyrus of Ani, Chapter LXXXI, "Becoming the Lotus")

The ancients would teach that prayer is not so much for "God, give me a new Cadillac", but a gentile aligning of ourselves to the Principle of Principles. As we turn toward the light of God in prayer, we are transformed more and more into God's image, - a process - like a lotus flower unfurling.

The state of being turned away from the light of the God and living as if the Principle of Principles does not exist, was referred to as being asleep. Therefore, when we finally awake to the love and glory of the Supreme Cause, it's like, "Wow! This is awesome!! Thus, "As if from a dream, I wake up laughing."

A great chapter of the ancient scriptures that discusses becoming aware of the glory of the Principle of Principles comes from the chapter entitled, "The Exe of God", Papyrus of Ani, Chapter XLII, "Awakening Osiris," Normand Ellis, translator.

The Eye of God

> The eye opens seeing old men, women and children. The eye recalls the beauty of the ordinary it sees me, therefore, I am. As such are we all created. It watches and pierces the heart. Who knows it's name? Call it love, creation, conspiracy. Call it an impossible sky hung with moons and stars. It is yesterday or tomorrow, a million years traveling. The sun circles and the hawk. We follow a flow. Thus looked upon the world receives its God.

I lived in the delta in a house of mud when I first felt its glance. I lived in its fire and never knew. I was asleep, dreaming blue dreams in the egg of the world. The eye opened and closed blinking once perhaps as it does every million years, and I came from unknowing into knowing. I left my hut yawning. I was naked in a bed of light. I shone like day. I opened like a purple flower at dawn.

I am in the eye of God, resting in its blue orb. Golden eyelids encircle me. Eyelashes grown like stalks of dark truth. I see what I never dared ~ beyond the bucket banging the well, beyond mountains pushing up dirt. Light shimmers in every blade of grass, God dances in every leaf, blue and gold fires leap from my pores. I shine in and out of life.

In this scripture, the ancient scribe uses the "Eye of God" as a metaphor to explain certain attributes of the Principle of Principles. It is interesting to note that Rene Descartes, the 17th century French Philosopher, in his search for certainty, believing the only thing he could not doubt was his own thinking, coined his famous "Cogito, ergo sum," or "I think, therefore I am." Descartes' statement is egocentric, whereas the Egyptian priest wrote, "[God] sees me, therefore I am." It may be argued that Descartes' egocentricity blocked his attunement to the Principle of Principles and therefore was unable to "hear" the "God within" and accordingly could not avail himself to the right-knowing that comes with attunement.

The Supreme God within, according to the Greater Mysteries was not a personality, as claimed by many religions today, nor a principle, as claimed by many in science, but rather the "Principle of Principles," the most abstract of the most abstract, so all inclusive as to be unsearchable to the mind of men.

According to this theology, therefore, from the immense Principal of Principles, in which all things casually subsist, absorbed in super-essential light, and involved in unfathomable depths, a beauteous progeny of principles proceed, all largely partaking of the ineffable, all stamped with the occult characters of deity, all possessing an overflowing fullness of good. From these dazzling summits, these ineffable blossoms, these divine propagations, being life, intellect, soul, nature and body depend; monads suspended from unities, defined natures proceeding from deities. Each of these monads, too, is the leader of a series which extends from itself to the last of things, and which while it proceeds from, at the same time abides in, and returns to its leader. And all these principles and all their progeny are finally centered and rooted by their summits in the first great all-comprehending one. Thus all beings proceed from, and are comprehended in the first being; all intellects emanate from one first soul; all natures blossom from one first nature; and all bodies proceed from the vital and luminous body of the world. And lastly, all these great monads are comprehended in the first one, from which both they and all

their series are unfolded into light. Hence, this first one is truly the unity of unities, the monad of monads, the Principle of Principles, the God of Gods, one and all things, and yet one prior to all.

(Thomas Taylor's introduction to his translation of "The Sixth Books of Proclus on the Theology of Plato.")

Many of the religious communities decry the polytheism of the ancient Egyptians and the Greek philosophers. However, the above quote from Thomas Taylor demonstrates their ignorance. These schools of thought firmly believed in the all powerful One Source, where all things came from. What appears to be an abundance of Gods to the ignorant is merely a way to describe, honor and worship certain aspects and progeny of the Principle of Principles, the One Unity.

The foregoing words of Taylor also discuss the principle of emanation and that from one source comes all else in a sequential order, not disorder. Monotheism, therefore, manifests itself through complex diversity, which, depending on the semantic interpretation may be called the "polytheism" of the Greeks, the "elohim" of the Hebrews, or even "all the angels and saints" of the Christian.

Thomas Taylor further discusses the principle of emanations. "For if whatever posses a power of generating, generates similars prior to the dissimilars, every cause must deliver its own form and characteristic peculiarities to its progeny; and before it generates that which gives substance to progressions far distant and separate from its nature, it must constitute things proximate to itself according essence, and conjoined with it through similitude. It is therefore necessary from these premises, since there is one unity principle of the universe, that this unity should produce from itself, prior to everything else, a multitude of natures characterized by unity, and a number the most of all things allied to its cause; and these natures are no other than the Gods."

This principle of emanation was adopted by the Gnostics and Kabbahlists. The theology/ philosophy of these groups held there were several main divisions between Source and matter. In Neo-Platonism these divisions are seven in number: 1) The Principle of Principles, which is un-searchable and is the same as the three-fold darkness of the ancient Egyptians; 2) Being, the first-third of the Triad of Cause; 3) Life; the next third; 4) Intellect; the last third of the Triad of Causes; 5) Soul, the top of the Triad of Generations; 6) Nature, the second point of the Triad of Generation; and 7) Body, the last point of the Triad of Generation. This is how the emanationist would view "creation" from the First Cause, to generation, which in turn would produce the physical based upon the defined order and procedure.

Everything begins with the First Principle, the Principles of Principles, the Supreme Monad, the One. From it are suspended the "divine principles" of Being, Life, Intellect, Soul, Nature and Body. Then from each of these principles are suspended progeny principles. These then in turn become principal (chief) principle of a successive line of suspended lesser or minor principles. The further down the line of succession, the greater the principle is subject to decay and transition. In other words, the greater the distance or interval between the "Divine Principle" and the subordinate principle, the lower the quality and function of that principle. Philo Judaeus used this same principle of degeneration to explain the mystery of the Adam of Genesis. To Philo, Adam was the Principle (chief) Monad of the human race. Therefore, human beings receive there function and qualities from Adamic Monad.

Philosophy teaches that all life is in a struggle for growth. This growth is the effort of life to return to its first Estate through the principle of generation. This is accomplished by the retracing of its degeneration as described above. It attempts to accomplish this by its efforts to include more and more of its environment into its reality of self-knowing. It is therefore the innate expression of the

inner life principle to refine and improve the vehicle it finds itself in. The "I" of the individual is ever changing and when aligned with the principle of virtue, ever perfecting. The "I" of one moment dies and a new "I" is born. This process continues *ad infinitum* until that life form returns to the Supreme Monad, the One, and ceases to exist. It was this principle of generation, the constant change of the "I", that prompted the ancient scribe to write in the Egyptian Scriptures:

Generation after generation, I create myself. It is never easy. Long nights I waited, lost in myself, considering the stars. I wage a battle against darkness, against my own ignorance, my resistance to change, my sentimental love for my own folly. Perfection is a difficult task. I lose and find my way over again. One task done gives rise to others. There is no end of the work left to do. That is harsh eternity. There is no end to be coming. I live forever striving for perfection. I praise the moment I die in the fire for the veils of illusion born within me. I see how hard we strive for truth, and once attained how easily we forget it.

(Papyrus of Ani, Chapter LXXX, "Becoming a Light in the Darkness")

The ancient penman describes how the principles of inertia also affects the principle of generation. Each "I", through striving for perfection also desires to remain in the familiar and more towards familiars (The Principle of Familiars), even if that which is familiar is more painful than the other. A practical example of the principle of familiars is the woman that stays in abusive relationship, not out of love, but because that is what is familiar, or woman who continue to date, "users", "losers" and "abusers."

The principle of generation holds that the Higher is always beckoning to the Lower to move up. The Higher is ever ready to lend a hand to help the lower break beyond the lower principle of inertia. The principle of the Higher aiding in the process of transformation is well demonstrated in the teachings of the monotheist Zarathustra, better known as Zoroastor. He taught his followers to worship only one God, Ahura Mazda, which is served by six Amesha Spentas, which are aspects of

divine being and are emanations of the Supreme Monad. The six are Vohu Manah, Asha Vahista, Khshatra Vairya, Spnta Armaiti, Hourvata and are known as the Ethical Virtue that span the gap from First Principle to that created, the abyss between the Holiness of God and human beings. These Amesha Spentas are "moral beings" who set examples for morality and therefore blaze a trail for those beings to follow. Zarathustra taught the philosophic principle that once a "thing" is done, it leaves a trace. It is therefore easier to do a second time, and this creates momentum. This principle, which is a variation of the principle of inertia, works for both good and evil, virtue and vice.

Philosophy teaches that the calling of the higher principle of generation is "stronger" than the cry of the lower principle of degeneration. This more powerful calling of Higher is well discussed in a fragment of a dialogue between the two principles in "De Arrna Animae," the mystical tract of Hugh of St. Victor.

> Tell me, what can be this thing of delight that merely by its memory touches and moves me with such sweetness and violence that I am drawn out of myself and carried away, I know not how? I am suddenly renewed: I am changed: I am plunged into an ineffable peace. My mind is full of gladness, all my past wretchedness and pain is forgotten. My soul exults: my intellect is illuminated: my heart is fire: my desires have become kindly and gentle: I know where I am, because my Love has embraced me. Also, because my Love has embraced me, I seem to have become possessed of something, and I know not what it is; but I try to keep it, that I may never lose it. My soul strives in gladness that she may not be separated from That which she desires to hold fast forever: as if she had found in it the goal of all her desires.

(Evelyn Underbill's "Mysticism", page 245)

Mystical experience described above shows the euphoria experience by the lower when relatively rapidly placed into the presence of the Higher. This feeling of well-being will be repeated

and may be experienced each time such leap is made to a higher plane. The feeling of dread will often accompany a similarly rapid degeneration into the lower.

It is only through philosophic principles that we may find "the goal of all [our Soul's] desires," the longing, the need to regain our first estate, the oneness with the Principle of Principles, the Law of God, which is One.

GAIUS JULIUS CAESAR

> Give me a state which is governed by a tyrant, and let the tyrant be young and have a good memory; let him be quick at learning, and of a courageous and noble nature; let him have that quality which, as I said before, is the inspirable companion of all the other parts of virtue, if there is to be any good in them."

The above quote is from a fictional dialogue between an Athenian stranger, Cleinias, a Cretan, and Megillus, a Lacedaemonian, in "Laws", one of the great works by Aristocles, most popularly known by the name of Plato. (Dover Publications, 2006, page 75) Plato lived from approximately 427 B.C. to around 347 B.C., some 250 years before Julius Caesar. However, his teachings not only shaped the life of Caesar, but influenced the entire Roman Empire at the height of its power.

Perhaps the greatest general and statesman of ancient Rome, Julius Caesar is the most recognizable of all personalities from the Roman Empire. Many scholars believe that ancient Rome would not have been nearly as relevant as it was without the efforts of Gaius Julius Caesar.

He was, however, not always thought of with such high esteem. In fact, the teenage Caesar would have probably been more comfortable hanging with the rich, spoiled brats of Beverly Hills 90210 than as a ruler of an Empire. However, before we can delve into the philosophy and methods Julius Caesar used to go from a rebellious rich kid to one of the greatest world leaders in all of history, we need to first look at the environment which allowed this to happen.

Antiquity of Rome

The most famous legend about the founding of Rome involves a set of twins and a wolf. According to the ancient Roman mythology, the twins Romulus and Remus were somehow abandoned and then adopted by a wolf. This wolf nursed and raised them. Romelus and Remus then formed a settlement on one of the hills near the Tiban River, known as Palatine Hill. Pursuant to this most popular legend, Rome was founded in 753 B.C. Recent archaeological digs have revealed mosaics dating back to the time of Julius Caesar that depicts the nursing of Romelus and Remus by the wolf.

Although not as popular, another legend originating in ancient Greece holds that Aeneas founded Rome after the destruction of Troy; Aeneas was a Trojan military hero. A third less popular myth holds that Romelus and Remus were descendants of Aeneas, thereby combining the two myths.

Although not disproving the Romelus and Remus legend, the archaeological evidence points in a different direction. It appears that the location of Rome was occupied as early as 1,500 B.C. during the Bronze Age. Most scholars agree that a continuous settlement was not established until approximately 1,000 B.C. These early settlers were probably from neighboring towns in Latium, and were called Latins. By the 8th century B.C. several of the other Roman hills were settled by iron-using Latins and Sabines.

About 600 B.C., Rome and several towns in Latium were conquered by the most powerful and organized group in the area known as the Etruscans. Under the control of the Etruscans, Rome rapidly grew from a village of shepherds and farmers to an important trade center with roads, public buildings and temples. Under the rule of the Etruscan King, Rome's citizenry became prosperous and powerful. In fact they grew so powerful, that in 509 B.C. the last king of Rome was

overthrown. The extreme negative attitudes toward the rule of the Etruscan monarchy by the Roman population affected decisions made by Julius Caesar centuries later.

The ensuing Roman Republic was not a true democracy. Initially only Patricians, the land owning upper-class were allowed to hold public office, interpret laws and act as the religious leaders. All of the other citizens were known as Plebeians and had few rights and were often oppressed. Under Patrician rule, Rome became a military power to be reckoned with. Rome formed an alliance with the "Latin League", a confederation of Latium Cities.

In 390 B.C., the Gauls invaded and burned Rome. Although not long after the burning of Rome, the Roman army defeated the Gauls; the Romans never forgot this indignity at the hands of the Gauls. Caesar would use the hatred of the Gauls to solidify his popularity some 330 years later. Rome turned its sights on its allies. In 338 B.C., the Roman army defeated its allies and disbanded the Latin League. Rome continued its ways and after victory over a Greek colony in southern Italy in 275 B.C., ruled almost all of the land of northern Italy.

During the 300's B.C. while the military conquests were going on, the oppressed Plebians were pressing hard for civil rights. By 287 B.C., the Plebians obtained equal rights under the law and could hold any office religious or secular. However, the economic chasm between the Patricians and Plebeians grew wider.

By 250 B.C., the population of Rome grew to approximately 100,000. The plunder from conquered lands funded massive public works including two aqueducts that flowed fresh water into the city. It was during that time that the Roman army would be tested in what would be called the three Punic Wars with Carthage, a strong military power and wealthy trading center in North Africa. During the First Punic War from 264 - 241 B.C., Rome conquered and seized the Mediterranean islands of Sicily, Sardinia and Corsica. The Second Punic War (218-201 B.C.) was

noted for the amazing accomplishment of Hannibal the brilliant general of Carthage who crossed the Alps with his army and war elephants. Hannibal won several major battles, but when he had the Roman army on the ropes, he inexplicably refused to attack Rome for the kill. The Roman army regrouped, and under the direction of Scipio, defeated Hannibal in 202 B.C.

The Second Punic War changed the completion of Rome. The peasantry fled the countryside and took refuge in Rome. In Rome they needed money, and sold their lands to the nobility. The nobles brought large numbers of slaves into the country to work the fields, which caused even more of the poor free peasants to move into Rome. Rome became a city of magnificent splendor and replete with horrendous slums. The Senate was preoccupied with foreign affairs and expansion of the empire and had little time to address the growing and worsening slums. The Third Punic War lasted only from 149 - 146 B.C. and resulted in Rome ruling the Mediterranean coasts of Spain and Africa.

At the time before Caesar's birth, Rome was a victim of its own success. With the Senate concentrating on the problem of the ever-growing empire, and no municipal government, basic necessities of food, clothing, shelter and water were left, for the most part to private individuals. The continuing influx of slaves and displaced freeman exacerbated the already overcrowded and deplorable *insulae* (ramshackle apartment buildings). Rome had little manufacturing or other industry to employ the mass of peasants, and unemployment was pervasive.

Two brothers, Tiberius and Gaius Gracchus attempted to help the poor by promoting the reestablishment of the small-farmer class by giving state-owned land to the poor and subsidizing food supplies. They obtained a certain measure of success in helping the poor, but the Senate disapproved of many of their ideas. Eventually, as was the custom too often used in ancient Rome, both brothers were assassinated.

Spurred by high unemployment and terrible living conditions, civil strife was the greatest threat to the Roman Empire at the advent of the life of Julius Caesar. The city poor and problems continued to mount with approximately 500,000 citizens receiving state grain. The rich got richer and it was status for the nobility to own a private army. This opened up some employment opportunities but greatly increased violence and established a new threat to the republic.

Early Years Of Caesar

The Julius Caesars liked to point out that their family tree may be traced back to the Goddess Venus. The "Julius" of Julius Caesar is the "extended family" or clan name, which at the time consisted of a number of Patrician families. "Caesar" was the family name of that particular family in the clan of "Julius". The name Caesar has become to signify a ruler who is extremely powerful, noble and supreme. The German "Kaiser", the Russian "Tsar" and the Islamic "quasar" were all derived from the sir-name Caesar. Our month of July is named after the clan name of Julius.

It appears that at the time of the birth of Gaius Julius Caesar, approximately 100 B.C., the Caesars were the only family left in the clan of Julius. The aristocratic family that Caesar was born into had both wealth and influence. However, scholars disagree on the extent of wealth and power by this group of Julius. Gaius Caesar, his father died when Caesar was 16 and he continued to live with his mother Aurelia, at least for another year.

A persistent legend is told about how when Caesar was a young man he was captured by Mediterranean pirates from the east. His captors told him that he will be killed unless they are paid a ransom of 20 talents. He is reported to have said, "only 20 talents?! I am worth more than 20 talents! I will give you 50 talents for my life!" A message was sent to Miletus to secure his ransom. During the messenger's absence he vowed to his captors that he would come back and hang them all. The pirates paid little mind to these threats, but within weeks after his release the entire group of kidnappers were captured and hung.

He married Cornelia when he was seventeen years old. Cornelia was the daughter of a powerful and wealthy man named Lucius Cornelius Cinna. Cinna was a close associate of a powerful and popular leader Gaius Marius. Caesar was associating himself with more and more politically powerful men. Even in his young adult life, Caesar was not afraid to defy authority and stand his ground. The aristocratic dictator of Rome, Lucius Sulla, ordered him to divorce his wife Cornelia. He flatly refused the dictator's order. Instead, he traveled to Greece where he studied the philosophy of the Greeks, including ethics, principle, logic, and oratory. While in Rome, Caesar would have been taught Greek philosophy which was appreciated by the Romans, but now that he was in Greece he could immerse and hone his mind with the wisdom of the Greeks. Eventually, Sulla gave Caesar a pardon and he returned to Rome, now with the skills to carry out his ambitions.

The Adult Caesar

While Julius Caesar was in his forced exile into the philosophic capital of the world, he would have studied the teachings of Plato and Aristotle. Although, in the first century B.C., the teachings of Aristotle were more popular than the teachings of Plato, Caesar would have studied Platonism. As indicated below, the actions of Caesar and his governing style point to a preference of the *a posteriori* reasoning method of Aristotelianism rather than the *a priori* reasoning method taught by Plato.

With Caesar's great political ambition and his need for power, he would have necessarily studied Plato's writings on the empire of Poseidon, the lost Atlantides, the Isle of the Sea. In *"Critias"*, Plato describes the ideal civilization in terms of Atlantean.

The descendants of Atlas, continued as rulers of Atlantis, and with wise government and industry elevated the country to a position of surpassing dignity.

While enjoying the abundance natural to their semi-tropic location, the Atlanteans employed themselves also in the erection of palaces, temples, and docks.

In the graves and gardens were hot and cold springs. There were numerous temples to various deities, places of exercise for men and for beasts, public baths, and a great race course for horses.

Plato then goes on to describe how the rulers of Atlantis were determined to conquer the world and how they used their resources in a manner to maximize their military might. The myth then goes on to describe the fall and sinking of Atlantis. Though slightly veiled in allegory, the epic makes it clear that the sinking of Atlantis was because the expansion of the empire and its commensurate power, glory and hubris blinded the twin eyes of wisdom and virtue.

Caesar would have studied how Plato, in his writings dreamed of that day when people would cease their petty squabbling in government. That a government not of the people or by the people would rule, but a government for the people. And that the state is truly fortunate whose ruler is a philosopher. This is because Plato taught that there will never be a time when the wisdom of people will equal the wisdom of a few wise men. Further, the state that is the most fortunate is the one who is ruled by the wisest of these wise men. Caesar would have most certainly agreed with Plato and believed that he is the man that Plato was referring to. It would not have just been Caesar's ambition to rule the Roman Empire, but his duty and destiny to rule.

Caesar would had also agreed with Plato when he read that there will rise a ruler of exceptional intellect that will, by divine providence, excel all others and elevated by newer and nobler codes of ethics, principle, morals, logic, and virtue to the supreme and wise ruler for the people.

Although Aristotelianism was more in vogue at the time of Caesar was in Greece, he no doubt loved reading Plato and thought that he was pointing directly at him.

Julius Caesar was acutely aware of the failings of the republican form of government in Rome. It was this government which allowed such abject poverty and the great indignity of the banishment of its greatest son to Greece. He would have read Plato as adamantly stating that only a tyrant could save and propel Rome to its rightful greatness.

> Then our tyrant must have this [virtue and temperance] as well as other qualities, if the state is to acquire in the best manner and in the shortest time the form of government which is most conducive to happiness; for there neither is nor ever will be a better or speedier way of establishing a polity than by tyranny.

(Plato's "Laws", page 76)

Caesar would have been convinced that the only way to save the republic was to eliminate the republic. This follows the sentiments of the much later Jewish statesman, Disrael, who stated, "The world is weary of statesmen whom democracy has degraded into politicians." Caesar would have studied and agreed with Plato's philosophy "that the change [to the perfect form of government] is best made out of a tyranny, and second, out of a monarchy; and thirdly, out of some sort of democracy, fourth, in the capacity for improvement, comes oligarchy, which has the greatest difficulty in admitting of such a change, because the government is in the hands of a number of potentials." (Ibid.) It is interesting to note that Plato thought that change out of oligarchy, where power is centered in a few, is the most difficult and, as discussed below, Caesar's first major push for power was with the First Triumvirate. This was an alliance between Caesar, Marcus Licinius Crassus and Gnaeus Pompey, all powerful and ambitious men.

Caesar would have also learned that, "without trouble and in no very long period of time, the tyrant, if he wishes, can change the manner of a state: he has only to go into the direction of virtue or of vice, whichever he prefers, he himself indicating by his example the lines of conduct, praising and rewarding some actions and reproving others, and degrading those who disobey." (Id., at 77) (Emphasis added)

Manly P. Hall summarized the teachings of Plato on the philosophy of government that Caesar necessarily would have studied:

> What is politics, however, but the philosophy of government? It is not universal law applied to the government of men, and should not the one who is made a ruler over others be conversant also with those sidereal forces by which the order of creation maintained? ...Yet, for the regulation of human affairs, what pattern is more sublime than the harmony of the celestial spheres or the innate orderliness of

crystal formation? <u>The science of mundane government fails because it ceases to be a science of government and becomes a science of personal interests.</u>

(Manly P. Hall, "Lectures on Ancient Philosophy", page 467) (Emphasis supplied).

Although the philosophy of Plato on government would have been well studied and understood by Caesar, it was Aristotelism that was the most popular at the time. Aristotle died some 140 years before Caesar spent his time in Greece, but his teachings would have had substantial sway on him.

Arguably, the two greatest conquers of the ancient world were Alexander the Great, who was king of Macedonia from 336 to 323 B.C. and Gaius Julius Caesar. It is interesting to note that Aristotle was a direct teacher of Alexander the Great and a teacher of Caesar through his disciples and the Peripatetics school.

When Alexander was fourteen years old, his father, Philip, then the king of Macedon wrote the following well-known dispatch to Aristotle:

Philip to Aristotle, Health:

> Know that I have a son. I render the gods many thanks; not so much for his birth, as that he was born in your time, for I hope that being educated and instructed by you, he will become worthy of us both and the kingdom which he shall inherit."

(John Williams, "The Life and Actions of Alexander the Great.")

Aristotle accepted King Philip's offer and traveled to Macedon and tutored Alexander for eight years. Alexander came to love and appreciate Aristotle as much as he adored his father King Philip. Alexander wrote that his father gave him being, but Aristotle gave him well-being. (Id.)

During one of Alexander the Great's military campaigns he heard that Aristotle had published one of his great discourses, (that would have been read and studied by Caesar). This so upset Alexander that he wrote to his mentor: "Alexander to Aristotle, health: You were wrong in publishing those branches of science hitherto not to be acquired except from oral instruction. What shall I excel others if the more profound knowledge I gained from you be communicated to all? For my part I had rather surpass the majority of mankind in the sublimer branches of learning, than in extent of power and dominion. Farewell." Aristotle responded to Alexander's letter stating that although the paper was published and available to the masses, nobody who did not hear Aristotle lecture could understand its true meaning. (Id.) Presumably, the disciples at the Aristotelian School who taught Caesar would have conveyed the more sublime meanings of Aristotelianism.

We do not know if Caesar was aware of the above letters to Aristotle, but certainly Caesar would have known of the awesome and amazing conquests of Alexander the Great. He would have known that Alexander conquered more of the known world than any other military leader, and that Aristotle was his personal mentor from his early teenage years to the time he began his conquests.

With ambitious as Caesar was, without question, he would have studied and devoured as much of the teachings of Aristotle as possible.

Philosophy Of Aristotle

In Thomas Taylor's introduction to his translation to Aristotle's "The Metaphysics", wrote, "The end of Aristotle's moral philosophy is perfection through the virtues, and the end of his contemplative philosophy on union with the one principle of all things."

Aristotle divided his philosophy into two parts: theoretical and practical. Theoretical philosophy included physics and logic, whereas practical philosophy included ethics and politics. Aristotle taught using dialetics, the same method as Plato before him and Socrates for Plato. Dialetics as a discipline may well have started with Socrates. It is a question-and-answer technique used for teaching and problem solving and derives from the Greek word meaning "to converse."

Caesar would have learned Aristotelian method of logic, which is the systematic pattern of reasoning and valid thought. He would have learned how to identify the essence of a problem and the proper steps necessary to evaluate options. He would have also learned the "Doctrine of Fallacies," which is a faulty process of reasoning using defective arguments. An example of this would be the fallacy of "arguing from authority" "womanizing and sexual promiscuity is the highest form of physical express, because Julius Caesar was a womanizer and sexually promiscuous." The knowledge of arguing with such faulty reasoning would have suited the ambitious Caesar well in his discussions/debates with the Senate. He would be able to recognize their faulty arguments and, where available, use the more subtle fallacies to his advantage. In other words, Caesar would have known why certain arguments are fallacies, why they appear to be valid and when such fallacy could be used to his advantage.

Aristotle based his philosophy almost exclusively on empirical observation. This is because he believed that the world of things perceived is the real world, which is contrary to the teachings of Plato. In Plato's Theory of Ideas, the world of "things" are imperfect copies of perfect "Ideas." To Aristotle, it was not necessary to have these transcendent Ideas. (Although in his theory, Aristotle would speak of *katholou*, which appear similar to Plato's Ideas.)

Caesar would have studied Aristotle's observation that man is above all a social being. Further, it is the overarching aim of man to direct his activities toward a satisfactory and good life; and subordinate aims are used to reach the superior aim. Aristotle observed that the market will control excess and therefore moderation will prevail. In other words no manufacturer will produce more product than can be consumed. However, with money, the illusion that wealth can be accumulated without limit harms the community and the individual and violates the principal of moderation. This is where Aristotle sees the need for controls to prevent this. He further observed that the ruler who needs to prevent private excess may himself become power drunk and become an oppressor, who then becomes hated by the oppressor. He said to break the cycle of excess, man needs relaxation, recreation, play or amusement.

Aristotle, like Plato, held that a leader must have virtue. He taught his star student, Alexander the Great to "feel that if he had not done a good deed he had not reigned that day."

To be certain, Caesar would have studied philosophies other than Plato and Aristotle. He would have studied Stoicism as created by Zeno of Citium who taught that the basis of happiness is virtue and to live in "agreement with oneself," everything else; including power, wealth and health are all completely indifferent.

Caesar would have also studied Epicureanism, which is basically the opposite of Stoicism. Epicurus held that the path to true happiness comes through the five senses; pleasure is the very essence of the happy life.

<u>Return To Rome And Politics</u>

In c. 78 B.C., Caesar returned to Rome after he was pardoned by the dictator Sulla. (Some scholars believe that Caesar was not pardoned, but rather returned to Rome after Sulla's death in 78 B.C.).

Not long after he arrived in Rome he traveled to Rhodes to study oratory. It was during this trip that the aforementioned kidnapping by the pirated occurred.

In 74 B.C., he raised a private army and fought against the king of Pontus, who renewed his war against Rome. Caesar and his wife Cornilia had one child named Julia. The same year he received his first elected position, 68 B.C., Cornilia died and so did Caesar's Aunt Julia. He used the public funeral forum to give a well received speech that was more political than eulogistic.

In 65 B.C., Caesar's big break came in his reach for power. He was elected the official who organized public games. As indicated earlier in this paper, Caesar studied the philosophy of public games while he was in Greece. This position raised his public profile and endeared him to the public. He excelled as a producer of games and three years later, buoyed by his public popularity, he was elected Praetor, just one notch lower than the Consul in rank.

In 60 B.C., after a failed attempt to disgrace Caesar by some leading aristocrat's, he formed the "First Triumvirate" which was an alliance between Caesar, Marcus Licinus Crassus and Ganeus Pompey. Crassus was a man of sufficient wealth and has considerable political power; Pompey was a great military leader and due to his military conquests was extremely popular with the people.

With this coalition of military and political bosses, Caesar's organization was a force to be reckoned with.

Using this powerful alliance, together with bribes and violence, in 59 B.C. Caesar was elected Consul, and shortly thereafter named Proconsul of three Northern Provinces. In that same year he married a woman named Calpurnia, daughter of Lucius Piso, who became Consul in 58 B.C., and his friend and ally, Pompey married Caesar's daughter Julia.

There is little doubt that Caesar agreed with Aristotle's ethics, which were based on the universe having a hierarchy in which everyone had a purpose. The rational being was the highest form of existence and the purpose of the lower forms are to serve the greater. Aristotle defended slavery on this basis and Caesar exploited this in bringing massive amounts of slaves from conquered lands and filling the ranks of the Legionaries with foreign conscripts. Instead of following Plato and his admonition that virtue must be applied to politics, he followed Aristotle, who said that the ethics of politics is different in theory and in practice. He held that law must dictate from virtue depending on the circumstances. Caesar no doubt read this as giving him a free reign to rule as he saw fit.

In the warrior society of Ancient Rome, Caesar knew that military victories were necessary for his rise to power. Even though he had no significant military training, in 58 B.C. he led the Roman Legionaries into Gaul and proved himself a military genius. These victories along with those in Britain in 55 and 54 B.C. solidified his public support.

In 49 B.C., his son-in-law and now ex-friend Pompey grew suspicious and jealous of Caesar. Pompey joined a group of powerful conservatives in the Senate, who ordered Caesar to relinquish his army. He refused and led 5,000 troops against his critics. Knowing this meant death if he failed, while crossing the river Rubicon, he explained, *"Alea Jacta Est"* (The die is cast.) To a casual observer, many of Caesar's political and military decisions were impulsive and illogical. Quite the contrary, Caesar was well trained in both the principles of deductive logic, which is used to draw new propositions out of existing premises, and those of inductive logic, which derives answers from facts that appear as supporting evidence. (These divisions of logic have been blurred over the years and have all but merged into to deductive logic.)

Even Caesar's critics do not deny that he had brilliant intellect and was extremely quick witted. With the training he received in systematic rational thinking using the principles of logic he would have been able to review a situation, military, political or other, logically process it and almost immediately determine a course of action.

Caesar's political and military decisions proved to be correct over and over. However, as a testament to Plato, any decision that does not include virtue will eventually fail. This lack of virtuous decisions by Caesar in bedding the men's wives repeatedly proved this principle. Caesar continually found himself in trouble because he could not keep his toga on.

His military decisions during the Roman civil wars against Pompey and his armies were exceptional. He defeated Pompey's forces at Pharsalus, on August 9, 48 B.C. Pompey fled to Egypt where he was murdered before Caesar arrived. Caesar traveled to Egypt with his army wintered in Alexandria, where he "met" a "woman of incomparable beauty and skills" named Cleopatra VII. From Egypt he began a brief military campaign in Asia Minor. After his victory there he sent the famous message to the Senate, *"Veni, Vidi, Vici"* ("I came, I saw, I conquered").

Cleopatra VII and Caesar turned Egypt with four hundred ships; the royal barge was 300 feet long and 60 feet high. Caesar was obviously impressed with what he saw and less than a year later he left in Egypt Cleopatra and their son named Caesarion ("Little Caesar").

In 44 B.C., Caesar was at the height of his power and had himself declared dictator for life. Mark Anthony offered him the crown of a king in public three times and thrice he refused. He no doubt remembered the hatred of the Roman people of the Etruscan kings.

Caesar did not forget his training in ethics and politics, and he pardoned all followers of his former friend, then enemy Pompey. These wholesale pardons included two men named Marcus Junius Brutus and Gaius Cassius.

On March 15, 44 B.C., Brutus, Cassius and sixty Senators, in a conspiracy, stabbed Caesar to death in the Senate building at the foot of the statue of Pompey. During the attack Caesar uttered the famous, *"Et Tu Brute?"* ("You too, Brutus?").

<u>Legacy Of Caesar</u>

The assassination of Gaius Julius Caesar may well have deprived Rome of its greatest hero. He set a pattern that was followed by the succeeding emperors, the next four to bear the name Caesar. However, not all of these emperors had the same training in ethics, principle and logic.

Much of the writings of Caesar are lost; those exant show the mark of a genius. Even though his writings that we have were written for propaganda, they are deemed by scholars to be of outstanding literary merit. His books on military affairs are studied in modern military academies.

His genius in various fields including generalship, administration, propaganda and policies in small measure is due to his training in principles of ethics, logic, and other philosophic disciplines which he received in his youth.

THE MEANING OF LOGIC

Logic is the study and implementation of the rules and essence of reasoning and of systematic patterns of valid thought. It is one of the six disciplines under which philosophy is commonly classified. Logic is often defined by what it is not. It is not the engagement of the faulty process of reasoning using defective arguments, called fallacies. Starting with Aristotle, logic has been called the "Doctrine of Fallacies." To date, there are over 125 separate fallacies identified, such as argument ad hominem, where a person's statements are rejected because of a logically irrelevant character defect: "You can't believe anything Tony ever says- about philosophy, because he drinks way too much."

Most importantly, logic is a system used to train the mind. A modern university education does not teach the student how to think logically. Ignorance is death, and intelligence leads to longer better life for all. True intelligence does not come from book learning, but rather from a balanced intellect, which only comes through logical thinking. Perhaps the greatest philosopher of all time, Pythagoras, stated that the training of the mind so as to make it capable of sustained logical activity is the first step toward realization.

THE SYSTEM OF LOGIC, THOUGHT OR IDEAS GOVERNING BUSINESS

Introduction

Business is not a mass of random acts of commerce, but rather a series of transactions governed by a system of logic, thought or ideas. Whether consciously or unconsciously those engaged in these transactions are also engaged in a system of logic, thought or ideas. The parties who are aware of this fact and/or have mastered this system are generally far and away the most successful. This is not to say that the most successful in business is the one who accumulated the most money. There should be and most often are considerations other than simple profit in business endeavors. The above considerations and the system of logic, thought or ideas as they relate to business will be discussed individually and collectively

Logic

Logic has been defined as the study and implementation of the rules and essence of reasoning and of systematic patterns of valid thought. The goal of logic is to train one's mind in the organization of intellectual faculties. The supreme philosopher Pythagoras, who taught over 100 years before the era of Socrates, Plato and Aristotle, said that salvation lies in the purification of the soul. This is accomplished through music and mental activity. Pythagoras further held that the mind must be trained to think logically. In his great work "Lectures on Ancient Philosophy," Manly P. Hall discusses this concept of Pythagoras.

> Supreme is his contemplative genius, Pythagoras differs from his eastern mentors in that he conceived the universal state to be attained through elevation of the mind rather than annihilation of thought procedure. As the first step towards realization, he accordingly taught the training of the mind so as to make it capable of sustained logical
>
> activity. The misconception is quite general that a common school education equips the mind for the profession of living, and, if supplemented by university training the individual is thereby qualified to question and debate intelligently the dictums of eternity. Modern education, is not founded upon strict rational procedure, hence

t he m ass o f h umanity i s n ot e ducated b ut r ather s upports i ts notions by the vain mumblings of archaic dogma. Unless first subjected to definite disciplines, the mind is incapable of rational functioning.

(Hall, "Lectures on Ancient Philosophy," page 121)

In order to fill this need to properly train the mind toward rational thinking, the ancient philosopher began formulating the principles of logic. At one time, logic was divided into the categories of inductive logic and deductive logic. Inductive logic looks to certain facts that appear as evidential support for certain conclusions. Deductive logic in which new propositions are formulated out of the inherent qualities of existing premises. This distinction has all but been abandoned and for the most part, the term logic and deductive logic are considered synonymous. Accordingly, in this paper, no distinction will be made between deductive and inductive logic.

The principles of logic had their origins in ancient Greece. Initially logic was divided into two topics: The logic of prepositions or sentences and the logic of noun expressions. The logic of prepositions are semantic in character as they deal with a part of speech. In this system of logic prepositional connectives are analyzed, ("if ...they""and,""or,""it is not the case that"). Prepositional logicians use p, q, r, s, ect. in their analytical formulea. The logic of noun expression is itself divided into two categories: names ("David,""Friend of John," ect.) and common nouns ("typist,""painter," "prisoner," ect.). Terms included in noun expression include "moves,""types,""runs," and "is the same as,""is,""every...is,""some...is not,""some...is," ect. In analyzing noun expression the logician will use a, b, c, d, ect. in their formulea.

Although the logic may have been used earlier, it was the Greeks in general and Aristotle in particular who formalized the first system of logic, which was the logic of noun expressions. In the 4th century B.C., Aristotle created the branch of formal logic known as syllogistics, which is contained in the logic of noun expressions. Syllogistics is the study of logical structures which make it possible to infer a conclusion from the premises.

In their philosophical pursuits, the Greeks loved the use of argument and proofs in their discussions. This set the stage for the development of the formal steps of the principles of logic. Aristotle was the first philosopher to write extensively on formal logic. His treatises were grouped in a collection entitled *"Orgonon"*. There are over a dozen books in this collection and carries the theme that logic is a tool for sharpening thought. Aristotle's books on logic include *"Categoriae,"* *"De interpretatione""Analytila priura"* (two books), *"Analytica posteriora"* (two books), *"Topica"* (eight books), and *"De sophistics elenchis."*

In Aristotlean syllogistics is divided into three components: 1) the theory of opposition, 2) the theory of conversion, and 3) the syllogistic proper. In *De interpretatione*, he writes extensively on the theory of opposition, which includes the affirmation and denial of universal and particular propositions. Examples of these are "every a is b" (universal affirmation) and "no a is b" (universal denial).

Analytica priora deals with the theory of conversions, which works with the logistical relationship that is maintained between a categorical proposition its opposite. Examples of the theory of conversion are 1) for all a and b, if every a is b, then some b is a, 2) for all a and b, if some a is b, then some b is a, and 3) for all a and b, if no a is b, then no b is a.

Also in *Analytica priora* also writes about Syllogistic proper, which Aristotle stated is a "propositional expression in which certain things having been laid down, something other than what has been laid down follows of necessity from their being so."

Aristotle stated that Syllogistic propositions are composed of terms, and accordingly, traditional logic must begin with an analysis of terms. The analysis of the connotation of a term is the definitions of that term. In other words, if the connotation of a term a includes that of b, the extension of b will include that of a.

There was little change in the field of logic from the ancient schools of philosophy until the end of the first millennium A. D. In the early eleventh century, St. Anselm of Canterbury made substantial stride in the advancement of the principles of logic. An Italian monk, he lived from A.D. 1033 to 1109 and became Archbishop of Canterbury. He funded scholasticism, and included Aristotelian logic into theology, and held that logic, reason and revelation are all compatible. Scholasticism is the term used to describe middle ages Christian philosophy and logic. It followed in large measure the parameters set down by Aristotle. Perhaps the most influential medieval logician was Peter

Abeland who lived from A.D. 1079 to 1142. The controversial French philosopher taught theology in the Catholic universities of Paris. He built on the "old logic" of Aristotle's *Organon* with new topics and methods, which he called "new logic."

In the 13th century logicians split into two schools of thought. One group held to the formal standards of Aristotelian logic while others took a more liberal view. Pope John XXI wrote one of the most authoritative texts on logic that was standard for the next 300 years.

The contributions to the field of logic by the Arabs cannot be overstated. During the dark ages of Europe, the writing of the ancient philosophers including Aristotle were lost and forgotten.

The Arab philosophers translated the books of Aristotle into Arabic and for the most part adhered to his methods of logic. The modern world can thank Avicenna for much of its philosophy

and theology. Avicenna was born in Persian in A.D. 980 and became perhaps the greatest medieval Islamic philosopher. He applied Neo-Platonist thinking to Aristotle and influenced medieval philosophers including St. Thomas Aquinas, who in turn continues to have significant influence on modern day Christianity. Before his death in 1037, Avicenna wrote extensively on the systems of logic.

Fallacies and paradoxes were favorites of the High Middle Ages logicians. Albert de Goot, also known as Albertus Magnus lived 74 years after his birth in 1206. He was the mentor of St. Thomas Aquinas and was said to have been "*magnus in magia*, major *inphilosophia, maximus in theologia*." He is credited with formulating several famous paradoxes including the man who swears falsely:

If someone swears that he swears falsely, then, if he swears falsely, what he swears is not true i.e., he does not swear falsely, but if he does not swear falsely, then what he swears is true i.e., he swears falsely.

If there is a father of modern logic it would be the 16th century anti-Aristotlian logician Petrus Ramus. Ramus considered logic the "art of discussing." He departed from traditional logicians in that he considered grammar and rhetoric to be concerned with matters of style and distinguished from logic. Ramus learned much from Rene Descartes, who was considered who the father of modern philosophy.

Frederick Copleston, SJ. writes of Descartes view of the system of logic thus:

> For he also believed that the use of the appropriate method would enable the philosopher to discover hitherto unknown truths. He did not say that scholastic logic is worthless, but in his view it "serves better for explaining to others those things which one knows...than in learning what is new." Its use is primarily dialectia Descartes' own logic, he says, is not, like that of the schools, "dialectia which teaches how to make things which we know understood by others or even to repeat, without forming any judgment on them, many words

> respecting those things which we do not know"; rather it is "the logic which teaches us how best to direct our reason in order to discover those truths of which we are ignorant."

(Copleston, SJ. "A History of Philosophy, Volume IV, Descartes to Leibnitz," page 71)

Ramus and his progeny, building on Descartes, mandated in any logical inquiry, obscure or uncertain terms should be defined, that only fully known terms should be used in definitions and that only obvious truths should be used in axioms.

Due to his extraordinary contribution to development of the principles of modern logic, some scholars believe that "Modern Logic" began with Gottfried Wilhelm Leibnitz, the German Rationalist.

On Leibnitz's, Copleston writes:

Leibnitz's logical theory, especially his view that all predicates are contained virtually in their subjects, seems difficult to reconcile with freedom, if by "freedom" one means something more than spontaneity. Leibnitz himself thought that it could be reconciled, and we are not, I think, entitled to speak as though he denied in his logical papers what he affirmed in his public writings. His correspondence with Arnauld shows that he was conscious of the fact that his subject-predicate theory, when applied to human actions, was unlikely to meet with a favorable reception, were it clearly set forth in a work like the "Monadology." And he may have allowed readers to attach a meaning to terms like "freedom" which they would hardly have been able to attach to them, had they been aware of his logical views.

(Id., at 287).

Philosophers began to apply logic more and more to mathematics after Liebniz. From Liebniz through the 18th century logic centered around a new approach to syllogistics and a search for mathematics that are capable of non-mathematical interpretation.

In the 19th century the French logician and mathematician Joseph Diez Gergonne spearheaded perhaps the greatest leap in the principles of logic since Aristotle. Gergonne returned to the Aristotelian tradition of logic. Of noun expressions and simplified and enhanced syllogistics.

Throughout the 20th and 21st centuries there were significant leaps in the systems of logic particularly in the area of mathematics. Since 20th century the view that mathematics is a continuation of logic with no black and white difference between them, but rather shades of gray, has been called "logicism."

Logic is indispensable in business but not purely theoretical abstract logic of say syllogism, but the more "practical" logic of "applied logic." In applied logic, the concepts listed above adopts them for use in concrete issues of a specific subject matter. The discipline of practical logic cannot be equated with applied logic, but rather is one of the branches of applied logic. Reasoning in the sciences, philosophy, business and everyday discourse is within the realm of applied logic.

An argument in applied logic is a discourse that considers evidence, valid or invalid to support some thesis. Invalid evidence is considered to be fallacious. Philosophers had spent considerable time identifying fallacies. There are now over 125 recorded fallacies. A few examples of these fallacies are as follows:

> The fallacy of irrelevant conclusion is committed when the conclusion changes the point at issue. (This was seen extensively in the Vice Presidential debate between Sarah Palin and Joe Biden.) This type of fallacy includes; 1) *ad hominem,* which is speaking against the man rather than the issue (instead of discussion nuclear arms as requested, an attack on Obama's voting record on funding for the troops was mentioned.); 2) *adpopulum,* as applied to the people's attitudes, likes and dislikes, instead of offering logical reasons or solutions for the premise ("I'm going to speak directly to the soccer moms out there." (Instead of addressing the question.)); 3) *ad verecundiam,* an appeal to all which seeks to secure the acceptance of the conclusion on the grounds of its endorsement by persons whose views are held in respect ("I spoke with Henry Kissinger and he agrees with me on ..."); 4) *ad ignorantiam,* an appeal to ignorance,

which argues that something is so since no one has shown it not to be so. ("I have been in charge of a 40 billion dollar pipeline project, the largest civil project ever undertaken in the United States." The pipeline has not been built is only in the planning stages, and may very well not be built.)

(In the above fallacies demonstrated in the Vice Presidential debate, I do not intend to "pick on" Governor Palin, to be certain, both she and Senator Biden extensively used fallacious arguments. The above is only intended to be used as an example and room does not allow for examples of both debates.)

A few other examples of fallacies are:

1) *petition principii*, begging the question or the fallacy of circular argument, which occurs when the premise is presumed, overtly or covertly, the same conclusion that is to be demonstrated ("Elizabeth Hastlbeck always votes wisely." "But how do you know?" "Because she always votes Republican."); 2) *post hock ergo propter hoc*, the fallacy of many questions, which consists of demanding or giving a single answer to a question when this answer could either be divided or refused all together, because a mistaken presupposition is involved ("Have you stopped kicking your dog?")

In order to have the greatest chance to succeed in business, one must have a clear understanding of logic and fallacies. Obviously, not all businessmen are classically trained philosophers. Often, the layman will refer to a logical thinker in business as someone who has good common sense. In the 1700's several business schools would call this "the ability to find your way out of the woods." In other words, the actor has the ability to assess the situation, move forward, continue the assessment of the ever-changing premises and continue to adjust the directions. This continued assessment and reassessment is the application of the principles of logic discussed above.

The businessman must be on the constant lookout for fallacies.

In determining whether to open a new liquor store in a certain area the proprietor needs to carefully evaluate all of the data. While reviewing the vicinity of the available location, a realtor may tell him that, "this is a great location. You better rent it today, Starbucks is opening right next door." The statement by the realtor is a variation of the argument *ad verecundiam* (an appeal "to awe"), which seeks acceptance of the greatness of the location because Starbucks, a company of great respect is opening next door. The fallacious inference by the realtor is obviously designed to awe the business owner by the name Starbucks Corporation, who has teams of professional location evaluators and the liquor store proprietor should ride on the expertise of the multi-national company.

However, just because Starbucks is a successful company does not mean that the location evaluation staff properly did their due diligence. Furtherore, the area may be great for a Starbucks, but terrible for a liquor store. The business man should not ignore the fact that a Starbucks is opening next door, but he should not base his decision solely on this fallacy. He needs to review traffic patterns, both foot and automobile traffic. The demographics of the neighborhood must be obtained. Is the rent appropriate for the traffic patterns and demographics.

Instead of rejecting the Starbucks fallacy, and ignoring the information, the proprietor should contact the location assessment department of Starbucks and ask if the manager will release their assessment data to him, which is fairly common in business.

Each individual in business, whether owner, manager or employee, must constantly be making decisions and each decision, great or small, should be based on logic. The most successful business man will ordinarily be the one who can rapidly base his decisions on logic. If he is trying to sell his new wind turbine to a customer he needs to know how to frame and phrase his sales pitch based on arguments designed using logic.

Business is simply a series of decisions be every member of the company's staff. There is no guarantee that a decision based on logic will always be the right decision, there may be the rare exception, but the vast majority of the time, the spoils will go to the logician.

Most philosophers agree that a modern university education does not prepare the mind to think logically. Business schools would do well to require a philosophy course in general, and logic courses in particular for all business majors.

Thought and Ideal

"Cogito, ergo sum" "I think, therefore I am" in the famous affirmation of Rene Descartes, who was born on March 31, 1596 in Touraine. In arriving at this statement, Descartes employed a technique known as methodic doubt. He reasoned that if he was created by an evil genius that kept him in a state of constant deceit, he could see that there is a possibility that he is being deceived into thinking that the propositions of mathematics are true. However, this, to Descartes, cannot apply to himself. "If I am deceived, I must exist to be deceived: if I am dreaming, I must exist to dream." (It is noteworthy that centuries earlier, St. Augustine made the point in *De libero arbitrio*, 2, 3, 7.")

"By the word thought I understand all that of which we are conscious as operating in us," wrote Descartes. He further stated that, "He who says, 'I think, therefore I am or exist,' does not deduce existence from thought by a syllogism, but by a simple act of mental vision, he recognizes it as if it were a thing which is known through itself." To Descartes, not only understanding, willing, and imagining are "thought," but feeling is also the same thing as thought.

Descartes did not use logic to prove his thesis, but only through itself. Some philosophers say that is where Descartes erred. "Descartes, it is said, had no right to assume that thinking requires a thinker. Thinking, or rather thoughts, constitute a datum; but the 'I' is not a datum. Similarly, he had no justification for asserting that I am 'a thing which thinks.'" (Copleston, "A History of Philosophy," page 95.)

Immanuel Kant, who was born on April 22, 1724 in Konigsberg, wrote extensively on thought, hi describing thought, Kant states that, "there are two sources of human knowledge, which perhaps spring from a common but to us unknown route, namely sensibility and understanding. Through the former objects are given to us; through the latter they are thought." Here Kant is saying that objects are given through a sense, thought through the understanding.

Johan Gottfried Herder was born in 1744 in Mohrungen, East Prussia. He differed from Descartes and Kant in defining thought. To Herder, Thinking is inward speaking, while speaking in the ordinary sense is speaking aloud or thinking aloud, whichever you like."

To Descartes, the principle (chief) attribute of spiritual substance is thinking. He further postulated that all spiritual substance is in some way always thinking. Accordingly, he wrote, "I have no doubt that the mind begins to think at the same time that it is infused into the body of an infant, and that it is at the same time conscious of its own thought, though afterwards it does not remember it, because the specific forms of these thoughts do not live in the memory."

Pursuant to the philosophy of Baruch Spinoza, who was born on November 24, 1632, the system of the mind and the system of the body are not two separate and distinct systems, but rather one system which can be looked at in two ways. The system can be looked at under the "attribute of thought", or under the "attribute of extension." He further stated that "To every mode under the attribute of extension there corresponds a mode under the attribute of thought," and this second mode he calls an "idea." Therefore, according to Spinoza, to every extended thing there corresponds and idea. It appears that there are two orders, the order of the bodies and the order of ideas. However, Spinoza said no, there are not two orders, but one order that can be looked at in two ways. "The order and connections of ideas is the same as the order and connection of

things." He explains this in stating that "man consists of mind and body" and that "the human mind is united to the body," but "the human body is man considered as a mode of the attribute of extension, and the human mind is man considered as a mode of the attribute of thought." Therefore, they are two aspects of one thing.

Spinoza held that the mind is the idea of the body. In other words, the mind is "the counterpart under the attribute of thought of a mode of extension, mainly, the body." Each of the many parts of the body has a corresponding idea. Accordingly, "the idea which constitutes the formal being of the human mind is not simple but composed of many ideas."

In addition to the "idea of the body," which Spinoza calls the mind, it is possible to have the "idea of the mind." This is because a human being can have the idea of an idea using his self-consciousness.

In Julien Offray de La Mettrie's short life (he lived from 1709 to 1751) he wrote several important works on thought and ideas. In "Natural History of the Soul," he submits that arising out of sensations is man's physical life of thought and volition, which is developed by education. He was a doctor who formed his philosophy, in large measure, based upon observation of himself and his patients. He was particularly intrigued as to how fever affected mind and thought. He postulated that "where there are no senses, there are no ideas; the fewer the senses the fewer the ideas; and where there is little education or instruction there is a paucity of ideas."

La Mettrie states that Descartes was wrong when he spoke of man in a dualistic manner (man is composed of a thinking substance, immaterial and free, and a body, which is an extended substance.) La Mattrie applied his thesis to the whole man and said Descartes should have done the same. He believed that mind/thought/ideas was interrelated with the body and could not properly function if the body was not properly functioning. His philosophy may have changed if he had met Steven Hawkings.

Kant spoke of ideas that are not related to the input of data from senses. He said these ideas transcend experience in that there are no objects which are associated with them. An example of this would be ideas of the soul as a spiritual principle and of the Principle of Principles. To Kant, the human mind has an innate tendency to seek unconditional principles of unity. By "unconditional," Kant meant that these ideas are not subject to the physical senses and understanding

A significant body of philosophic work adheres to the theory of innate ideas. The theory of innate ideas holds that there were ideas at the very beginning, that were not any intervening circumstances which produced or influenced the idea. Empiricism is the opposite view. It holds that all ideas are derived solely from sensory experience, and if necessary, using observation and experience.

John Locke, who lived in England from 1632 to 1704 is credited with being the father of British Empiricism. He decided to research the source and extent of human knowledge. Copelston comments on Locke thus,

> In connection with the first problem, the source of our knowledge, he delivers a vigorous attack on the theory of innate ideas. He then attempted to show how all the ideas which we have can be explained on the hypothesis that they originate in sense-perception and in introspection or, as he put it, reflection. But though Locke asserted the ultimately experimental origin of all our ideas, he did not restrict knowledge to the immediate data of experience. On the contrary, there are complex ideas, built up out of simple ideas, which have objective references. Thus we have, for example the idea of material substance, the idea of a substratum which supports primary qualities, such as extension and those "powers" which produce in the percipient subject ideas of color, sound and so on. And Locke was convinced that there actually are particular material substances, even though we can never perceive them. Similarly, we

have the complex ideas of the casual relation; and Locke used the principle of causality to demonstrate the existence of God, of a being, that is to say, who is not the object of direct experience. In other words, Locke combined the Empiricist thesis that all our ideas originate in experience with a modest metaphysics.

(Copleston, "A History of Philosophy," Volume IV. page 26)

Locke wrote that there are only simple ideas. There are "nothing but several combinations of simple ideas. ... It is by such combination of simple ideas, and nothing else, that we represent particular sorts of substances to ourselves." For example, "the idea of the sun, what is it but an aggregate of those several simple ideas, bright, hot, roundish, having a constant regular motion, at a certain distance from us, and perhaps some others?"

Thought and idea in business are a direct result of some goal or ideal for the actor, whether owner, manager or employee. Any action taken is the direct result of thought and idea. No one can walk across the room or pick up a pencil without first having the idea to accomplish the act. So, what actions should be taken in business, and *a priori*, what thoughts and ideas should the individual have?

To answer that question we need to look to the company's mission statement, its goals and ideals. The company mission statement is the overarching reason for its existence. It could be simply to maximize profit (although Plato would say that such a singular reason for the company's existence is detrimental to the company, its owners and society); the mission statement could be to maximize profit while providing the highest possible day care services available; or, in a soup kitchen it might be "to feed the poor."

Whether the mission statement is grand or subdued, those principles of the company that formulated that statement did it based on a complex idea or a collection of complex ideas, which themselves are a collection of simple ideas.

Ideals then can be set. The ideal is something beyond and above which the individual strives for. Next in line would be a series of individual and collective goals. The ideal of the accounting department may be to provide timely and accurate information. The goal of Jessica in the accounts payable department may be to have all of the invoices from General Electric processed by the end of the week.

No company, individual or business is autonomous. The nature of business and commerce necessarily requires interaction and communication with others. If a proprietor who is the only employee makes custom ash trays, he still needs to obtain new material and supplies and he needs to sell his product. This requires communication. All communication is based on words or actions, which would include writing, graphs, display advertising, etc. All words or actions are thoughts expressed. Every action and every word begins with a thought or idea. Business simply would not exist without ideas.

Institution plays an important role in business. I an using the term institution here as meaning an "educated" institution. An example of this is a captain of a deep sea fishing vessel that has spent thirty years on the sea. If he runs into a situation he has never encountered before on the ocean, he seems to know exactly what to do, even in a life or death situation. His institution educated by a lifetime on the sea generates the necessary thoughts or ideas almost immediately. If you put an accountant from Wisconsin on that same boat in that same situation, even though he may have a brilliant intellect, he will have no clue what to do.

Without thought or ideas there could be no commerce, no business, no staff and no existence.

Cogito, Ergo Prossum Negotium, (I think, therefore I am able to do business.)

JEAN-JACQUES ROUSSEAU

Early Years

One of the most influential philosophers of modern times is the great Jean-Jacques Rousseau. He was born the son of a watchmaker on June 28, 1712 in Geneva, Switzerland. His mother died during childbirth and he was taught by his father that the Rousseau's were destined for greatness. The Hubris of his father continually got the best of him. He married an upper-class woman and began to wear a sword. Someone dared to insult him and he drew the sword to protect the Rousseau honor. Unfortunately, his actions were illegal and he had to flee Geneva to avoid imprisonment. Young Rousseau was only ten years old at the time and was forced to live with his mother's family where he was humiliated and treated poorly. In 1725 at the age of thirteen, he was apprenticed to an engraver for a period of five years. Three years into his apprenticeship, when he was sixteen years old he ran away.

He was extremely fortunate to meet a clergyman in a nearby town, the Priest of Confignon, who introduced him to a benefactress by the name of Baronne de Warens. He lived in her home and was employed as her steward; he was more like a son to her than an employee. In 1728 Rousseau, under the prompting of Warens, was baptized into the Roman Catholic Church. In one of his later books, *Confessions*, he wrote most unfavorably of his time as a catechumen.

Warens insisted that the boy become properly educated. Under his guidance, he went from a boy who never attended a formal school, to a highly educated man, a musician, and a philosopher.

It is interesting to note that the woman that had such a great influence in shaping the young Rousseau's career, was a woman with a past. Before arriving at Savoy, where she met Rousseau she was married to a man of means. She stripped him of his money, converted to Catholicism, ran away with the gardener's son, and set herself up as Catholic missionary concentrating on the conversion of "young male Protestants." Rousseau would later write that he was greatly troubled by Waren's moral character. This distress continued even during the period when Rousseau and Warens were lovers. Although Rousseau does not write about how this affair affected his thought, it must of had an impact on his core values.

Early Career

In 1742, Rousseau moved to Paris where he met another young philosopher by the name of Denis Diderot, who was one year his junior. To be certain, Rousseau lived at an auspicious time for a philosopher. The writings of Rene Descartes and Thomas Hobbes, who died in 1650 and 1679 respectively, were still fresh and respected. He was a contemporary of great philosophers with names like David Hume (1711 - 1776); Francois Marie Arouet de Voltaire (1694 - 1778); Immanuel Kant (1724 - 1804); Johann Gottfried Herder (1744 - 1803); and the aforementioned Denis Diderot (1713 - 1784), to name a few; along with the Austrian Wolfgang Amadeus Mozart (1756 - 1791) who based his operetta *Bastien und Bastianne* on Rousseau's c. 1752 *Le Devin du Village.*

In 1743, one year after moving to Paris, he transferred to Venice as the secretary to Comte de Montaigu, the French ambassador. There was significant friction between the two men and the following year Rousseau was fired and he returned to Paris.

In 1745, he met Voltaire, and in 1749 his friend Diderot asked Rousseau to write articles on music for the publication *Encyclopedia,* of which Diderot was editor. *Encyclopedia* was an important intellectual periodical that was very anti-religion in nature with contributing writers that were philosophers and religious reformers. Due to his eloquence, forceful writing style and well reasoned views, he quickly became one of the favorite writers of *Encyclopedia's* readership.

Rousseau was as adept at composing music as he was at writing essays. His operas were so highly regarded by the king and his court that Rousseau was apparently offered and turned down a lucrative position as composer retained by the crown.

Major Works

In the mid 18th century, the academy of Dijon established an essay contest seeking writings on whether the advent of arts and sciences had improved or corrupted humanity. In 1750, Rousseau published his prize winning essay, *Discours sur les sciences et les arts (A Discourse on the Sciences and the Arts)*. He immediately became a famous philosopher and the toast of France. He was known throughout the circles of the upper-class and academians for his intellect. In his essay, Rousseau argued that advancement of society and civilization have not enhanced humankind, but rather was the cause of its decay. He did not say that society and civilization are inherently evil, but that they have taken the wrong direction. The idea that the history of man's life is the history of decay was not new. That philosophy was written about by Roman Catholic philosophers since the time of Thomas Aquinas in the Middle Ages and even the Gnostics of the first century. However, where Rousseau differed was that he believed in the inherent goodness of man. In fact, he made this principle the foundation of his essay. Oddly enough, many scholars believe that Rousseau received the inspiration for this essay from his "former" lover and mentor Madam de Warens.

The idea of man's core goodness caused him to stand contrary to both conservatives and radicals of his day. Accordingly, the ideas discussed in the *Discourse* were met with strong opposition from many of the established philosophers. For several years after the publishing of the essay, Rousseau remained as a writer for *Encyclopedia*, which only enhanced his reputation.

The Dijon academy offered another prize for an essay answering the question, "What is the origin of inequality among men." Rousseau entered this competition with his *Discourse sur Vorigine de l'inegalite (Discourse on the Origin and Foundation of Inequity among Men)*. He did not win the prize, but nonetheless received critical acclaim after it was published in 1758. In this essay, Rousseau stripped away all society and civilization from man showing that man is naturally good.

He begins the *Discourse* by identifying two major type of inequality, natural and artificial. The first he places things like size, strength, intelligence, etc. In the latter he places all of the aspects of society. In his paper he attempts to explain the inequalities of the societal aspects of man. Unlike Aristotle, but in agreement with Hobbes, Rousseau suggests that original man was not a social being, but rather entirely solitary, he was happy and healthy, content and free. It was only after society began to form that the oppression of one man by another began. Accordingly, Rousseau does not blame nature for man's current ills, but rather society.

In his paper, Rousseau postulates that men initially built primitive dwellings which led to cohabitation between men and women; thus the family unit was born. This initial phase of society was referred to as a "Nascent Society" and was good. However, jealousy entered society, and "keeping up with the Jones" was the ruin of civilization. He argues that the further introduction of property was a "fatal" concept of mankind. This is because with property, man must institute laws and government to protect property "rights." He referred to this as one of the "horrors" that result from diverging from the thought that the earth belongs to no man.

In 1754, Rousseau grew tired of Paris and decided to return to Geneva. In his efforts to regain his Genevian citizenship he renounced Roman Catholicism and was received back into the Protestant church. In order to endear himself to the citizens of Geneva, he wrote a dedication for his second *Discourse* to the republic of Geneva. In his paper he trashes society, and in an effort to soften this condemnation, in the dedication he praises Geneva for maintaining the perfect balance of "the equality which nature established among men and the inequality which they have instituted among themselves." Later that year he returned to Paris and sent a copy of his *Discourse on Inequality to Voltaire*, who wrote and thanked him for sending a copy of his "new book against the human race."

Retirement

From 1756 to 1762, Rousseau lived in "retirement" on the country estate of a friend, Mme d'Epinay, near Montmorency. Mme d'Epinay loved to show off her guest with continued social gatherings. He then moved to a cottage called Montlouis for greater seclusion. He wrote and published extensively during this period of self imposed exile.

In 1758, he published an article in response to an article that appeared in *Encyclopedia* authored by Jean d'Alembert in which he had Geneva for banning theatrical performances. Rousseau's paper was entitled *Lettre a d'alember sur les spectacles (Letter to Monsieur d'A Lembert on the Theatre)*.

In 1761, Rousseau published his novel entitled Julie: ou, la nouvelle Heloise *{ Julie: or, The New Elouise)*. His novel deals with complex love between noblemen and commoners. It illustrates how people can find love and happiness in the family unit instead of the state- private life versus public life. It also incorporates one of Rousseau's principles that "men should rule the world in public life, and women should rule men in private life." This was the most widely read of all Rousseau's writings, and because it was a novel, was not subject to the same type of scrutiny as his other works,.

The following year, in 1762, he published two of his famous and controversial works, *Du contrat social (Social Contract)* and *Emile*, which was his book on education. *Emile* disclosed the improper moral conduct of the pious members of the French Parliament, and *Social Contract* attached the morals of the Calvinists of Geneva. The ire of the establishment was raised in both Geneva and Paris. His books were ordered burned and Rousseau arrested. He escaped from France and took temporary refuge in Switzerland. Due to the oppression he felt in Switzerland, in 1763 he renounced his Genevian citizenship.

He then decided to move to Berlin, but instead, in January 1766, he traveled to England with his friend Davis Hume, who promised him sanctuary and a place to write.

Hume secured a guarantee of a pension from King George III. However, he believed that the intellectuals of England, including Hume, were mocking and ridiculing him. He decided to leave British soil. In May 1766, he returned to France, and despite his open arrest warrant, in 1770 he returned to Paris. Unlike his friends Voltaire and Diderot, who both spent time in jail for their writings, Rousseau was never arrested.

In 1768 at the age of 56, he finally married "the only person he could rely on", a lady-friend by the name of Therese. In the first years of his life, Rousseau primarily wrote autobiographical writings to support his positions taken in his earlier writings and illustrate where his accusers and adversaries were wrong. The most famous of these writings is *Confessions*, which was somewhat patterned after St. Augustines' *Confessions*. This work which has become a classic in philosophic literature, was published in 1782, four years after Rousseau died.

Legacy

Although Rousseau was not the most academic of modern philosophers, he was nonetheless one of the most influential. His opinions and writings stretched the boundaries of ethical and practical philosophy.

In contrast to the political philosophies of Niccolo Machiavelli (1467 -1527) and Thomas Hobbes (1588 - 1679), which concentrated on the absolute power of rules and kings, Rousseau centered on the freedom and equality of citizens. His political philosophies were influenced heavily by the Bristol born John Locke (1632 - 1704), however, Rousseau, favored the "general will" over individual rights. To Rousseau, the state needs to be a moral entity with: 1) an ethic and life that is in harmony with its people, 2) with public laws in accord with the general will, and 3) a firm ultimate goal of liberty and equality of the people.

Further, if the state were to disenfranchise its citizenry, it is not only the fight of the people, but their obligation to rebel against the government.

His influence stretched beyond political philosophy and he influenced people's taste in music and the arts. His writings changed the way people viewed their children and how they were educated; he taught that in relationships, love and friendship was better than polite restraint. Throughout his career, he kept coming back to the concept that man is good by nature and has been corrupted by society. Perhaps his greatest legacy is his lasting influence on people's attitudes and faith in representative democracy, civil liberties and the innate goodness and dignity of man.

BENITO MUSSOLINI
AND THE DOCTRINE OF FASCISM

Introduction

When Fascism is mentioned, the first name to come to mind is Benito Mussolini, and with good reason. Mussolini himself stated near the end of his career, "Fascism is Mussolinism...what would Fascism be, if I had not been?" (See Herman Finer's Mussolini's Italy) Mussolini's faults were legionary, diverse and substantial, yet any condemnation of him should be tempered with admiration. His rise to power and his influence on the people of Italy is well worthy of study.

Early Years

Mussolini was born on July 29, 1883 in the town of Predappio, Italy. He was the eldest in a family of modest means. His father was a blacksmith by trade and a part-time socialist journalist; his mother was a school teacher. The entire Mussolini family lived in a small decrepit apartment called *apalazzo*. In later years Mussolini would speak fondly of his meager beginnings and call himself a "man of the people." His father spent most time in the taverns drinking instead of tending to his blacksmith responsibilities and spent much of the little money he had on his mistress.

Mussolini was an aggressive child who has been described as a bully, moody, unruly and disobedient. In today's society he would have no doubt been diagnosed as having Attention Deficit Disorder and prescribed a cocktail of drugs including Ritalin.

The instructors at the local school could not control the troubled child and he was sent to boarding school at Faenza, Italy, run by a strict order called the Salesians. He was expelled after stabbing one of his fellow students with a penknife and assaulting one of his instructors. He was sent to a school in Forlimpololi, Italy for troubled students, and was promptly expelled for a yet another penknife stabbing of a student.

In spite of his violent belligerent manner, he was able to complete school and obtain teaching credentials in his late teens. He knew almost immediately that being a schoolmaster was not for him.

At the age of nineteen he quit his job and left for Switzerland with no money and few belongings. He would later write that in the first few months in Switzerland all he had in his pockets was a nickel medallion of Karl Marx.

In describing Mussolini, most scholars will use words like, rebel, egoist, extremist, opportunist, and self-centered. All of this is no doubt true, but he was also a man deeply interested in philosophy. In the early time in Switzerland, what little money he had he spent on books and writings of the great philosophers including Kant, Spinoza, Kropotkin, Nietzsche, Hegel, Kautsky, Sorel, and many others. To be certain, he would keep what he liked and discarded the rest. Although all students do the same to one degree or another, this left Mussolini with a disjointed hodgepodge philosophy with no firm direction. What this method of study allowed him to do was to switch sides in the middle of a discussion and argue opposing sides with equal fervor. And he saw nothing wrong with such an about-face. This attribute would serve him well in his career.

While still in Switzerland he honed his skills in oratory and gained a reputation as a powerful political journalist and public speaker. He used his new found expertise in propaganda in furtherance of a trade union. He proposed a strike and was quick to recommend and use violence on friend and foe alike. He was arrested and imprisoned several times for his calls for vengeance and violence.

In 1904 at the age of twenty-one, he returned to Italy and became a schoolmaster. He said that during this period he lived a life of "moral deterioration."

In 1909, he married the sixteen year old daughter of his father's mistress (not his half-sister) named Rachel Guid, and moved into a small apartment.

Politics and Fascism

Soon after his marriage, Mussolini immersed himself totally in political endeavors. The Italy that he found himself in was anything but a happy, healthy, and prosperous century. He, as well as most Italians, found themselves living in poverty with no end in sight. The government seemed to only care about the wealthy influential people and gave little hope for the masses of the poor.

At the time Italy had a Constitutional Monarchy and a Parliament similar to that in England. However, unlike the British Parliament, no one party could come near a majority with power shared by the Socialists, Liberals, radicals, Republicans, Christian Democrats, Nationalists, and others. Political coalitions were, like the government at large, unstable and ineffective. There was little stability and less confidence in the Italian Government.

It was upon this backdrop that Mussolini made his move. At twenty-six years of age his status with the Socialist party, the most powerful of the various parties at the time, led him to the editorship of *Il Popolo* and a party office. An addition, he was editor of another socialist paper *La Lotta di Classe*, and later *Avantil* The office paper of the Socialist party.

Shortly before Italy's involvement in World War I, Mussolini was an anti-militarist and anti-nationalist. He used the power of the press to violently oppose Italy getting involved in WW I. However, he read that Karl Marx stated that social revolution usually follows war, and abruptly

changed his position. He began writing articles and giving speeches violently in favor of war. He resigned from *Avantil* And was forced out of the socialist party. In his own words, his new philosophy was. "From today onwards we are all Italians and nothing but Italians. Now that steel has met steel, one single cry comes from our hearts - *Viva L'Italial*" The Fascist battle cry was born.

In May 1915, Italy entered the war and six months later so did Mussolini. He served as a sharpshooter until his wounds caused him to leave the army in 1917. He returned from the war a complete anti-Socialist and shortly began advocating the need for a powerful dictator ~ "a man who is ruthless and energetic enough to make a clean sweep."

The political scene was extremely volatile between 1919 and 1922. In 1919, Mussolini had no party affiliation and no political base, so he started *Fasci di Combattimento*, a fascist veterans' organization. In the next election he failed to secure even one seat. It appeared that the Fascist party would have a silent end.

Almost one year later toward the end of 1920, Mussolini and the Fascists got their big break. General strikes were called in Italy and factories were taken over by workers. The government was slow to react. Mussolini and his "black shirt" veterans jumped into action and put down the "social threat" with brutality and intimidation. His systematic shootings and beatings of the demon socialists was welcomed by the upper and middle class property owners. In 1921, Mussolini's fascists held 35 seats in the national legislature.

In the fall if 1922, Mussolini toyed with the idea of forming a coalition government with certain other parties, but instead decided to march on Rome. Approximately 26,000 Fascists followed him to the capitol. King Victor Emmanuel for some reason failed to mobilize the military to crush the Fascist coup, and instead agreed to Mussolini's demands to form a Fascist government

in Rome. On October 31, 1922, the once troubled teen became the youngest "Prime Minister" in the history of Italy.

The Fascists continued their waves of violence and continued to gain power. By 1926 there was nothing left of Parliament except an empty shell. In 1928, the Fascist Grand Counsel became the official central governing body with Mussolini as the president of the thirty member counsel. The Fascist ruled all and Mussolini ruled the Fascists.

Ideology

One of the most unique features of Fascism was the idea of the "Corporative State." In this concept, the central government had political control over the private sector. The economy was to be set up similar to capitalism with private property, employers, and employees, but the functions of the economy would be controlled by government regulation and supervision. It appears, in many respects to be the same type of regulation and supervision of the economy that many politicians are advocating now in the United States in light of the current economic crises.

The corporate state laws however attempted to control every aspect of the economy. Strikes and lockouts were specifically outlawed. Corporations were divided into two "bodies." One for owners and one for employees. Before long, only members of the Fascist party were allowed to have voting rights in the corporate bodies.

These corporate bodies were designed to give the Fascists full and complete power over wages, labor disputes, production, prices and quality. In essence, as complete power over the economy as they had over politics.

The control over the political and economic structures were joined into a "chamber of deputies," obviously all Fascists. In 1939, this gave way to the "chamber of faces and corporations", which they controlled all things in Italy.

Much like Mussolini's personal disjointed philosophy, it is difficult to identify a complete statement of fascist ideology. In 1932, Mussolini did publish a document entitled "Political and Social Doctrines," which attempted to identify what Fascism is all about.

First of all, Fascism abhors liberalism, socialism, and democracy because they are geared toward the individual instead of the state and tend towards pacifism instead of aggression. The Fascist sees life as a struggle and the spoils go to the most aggressive and violent.

> "...Fascism above all does not believe either in the possibility or utility of universal peace. It therefore rejects the pacifism which masks surrender and cowardice. War alone brings all human energies to their highest..."

Conquest of other states, and the push for an empire are ideals to follow.

The state is everything, and controls everything - political, economic and moral. The individual must be completely loyal to the state; nothing less will be tolerated.

> "...for the Fascist, all is comprised in the State and nothing spiritual or human exists - much less has any value - outside the State. In this respect Fascism is a totalizing concept, and the Fascist State - the unification and synthesis of every value - interprets, develops and potentiates the whole life of people. No individuals or groups exist outside the State..."

Fascism may be summed up as an ideology with the state as the be all and end all. It rules by discipline, intimidation and violence. Individual rights are unimportant and absolute loyalty of the individual to the state is all that will be tolerated.

The need for a Fascist empire caused Mussolini to invade Ethiopia in 1935. His desire to revive the Roman Empire led Mussolini into his attack on Spain, Albania and his partnership with Germany in World War II.

The Fall

Mussolini at first believed his own press and thought he was an equal partner with Hitler. This didn't last long and he soon realized that his opinion had "only a consultative value." During meetings with Hitler, the German leader would extol a list of German victories and list the Italian defeats. Mussolini abhorred the fact that his ally would not inform him of the German war plans -The invasion of Romania and the Soviet Union were commenced without any notification to Mussolini.

Under Mussolini's leadership the war was a fiasco from beginning to end. On July 24, 1943, the Fascist General Council, which had not met in years, overwhelmingly voted to dismiss Mussolini from office.

He defied the order and was arrested. He was eventually transported to a hotel in the Abruzzi Mountains. German Special Forces crash landed a glider behind the hotel, rescued Mussolini and transported him to Munich.

At Hitler's urging he formed a new Fascist government in Northern Italy, but it had virtually no authority and no military. He tried to raise a group of loyal men to make a final stand, but could only get a few men to follow him. He tried to escape to Germany disguised as a German soldier, but was recognized. Mussolini, along with his mistress Claretta Petacci, were shot and killed.

His death was greeted by most of the Italian people with jubilation. They blamed him for dragging them into an expensive and devastating war and for all of their current ills. Mussolini died in disgrace.

MOHANDAS K. GANDHI
AND NONVIOLENT RESISTANCE

Persons in power should be careful how they deal with a man who cares nothing for sensual pleasure, nothing for riches, nothing for comfort of praise, or promotion, but is simple determined to do what he believes to be right.

These prophetic words were written by Gilbert Murray in an article in the Hibbert Journal regarding Mohandas Gandhi published in 1918, before Gandhi became a prominent political figure.

Early Years

Mohandas Karamchand Gandhi was born on October 2, 1869. He was the youngest child of his father's fourth wife (his first three wives died.) His father Karamchand Gandhi was the dewan or head administrator of Porbandor, the capitol of a small State in Western India. His mother Putlibia was extremely religious, cared nothing for material assets and would spend much time nursing the sick. Neither parent had any real formal education, but his father was very adept at dealing with the British who were in control of India at the time.

The main religion of the Gandhi household was Vaisnavism, which centered on the worship of the Hindu Savior god vishna, together with Jainism, an ancient Hindu religious sect, which teaches nonviolence and that everything in the universe is eternal and has its purpose.

As a young boy, Gandhi did not appear to have any special qualities. He was a small child and although not dull, did not seem to possess any type of superior intellect. In short, he seemed to be the average youth growing up in the late 19th century India. He started school at the age of

seven and did so without much enthusiasm. He did not spend much time with his schoolmates and in his words, "I literally ran [home] because I could not bear to talk to anybody. I was even afraid lest anyone poke fun at me." He was concerned about being teased because of his small size, his huge ears and because he thought he was "a very poor student." One of the surviving reports from school states that Gandhi was "good at English, fair in Arithmetic and weak in Geography; conduct very good, bad handwriting."

He had his share of youthful rebellion, and admitted to "secret atheism, petty thefts, furtive smoking," and perhaps the most surprising of all, "meat eating." He soon decided to stop these delinquencies; he vowed "never again." and kept his vow.

He was married at the ripe age of 13, not unusual for the late 1800's in India. He took a year off of school due to his nuptials, then returned and finished his schooling. In 1887, Gandhi barely passed his entrance exam and started college. The teaching was in English instead of his native language, and he had difficulty following the lectures.

He contemplated becoming a doctor, but with pressure from his family, decided on law. In 1888, he vowed to his mother that he would not touch wine, women or meat, and left for England to study law.

During his three years studying law in England, he also studied religions. He read the Bible for the first time and also the Bhagavad Gita, the poetic teachings of Hinduism. He met many intellectuals, philosophers and theologians. He spent time with Annie Besant who was a theosophist, which was a group formed by Madam Blavatsky. She exposed Gandhi to a blend of Hinduism and spiritualism.

While in England, he was still self-conscious about his small size and big ears. In order to attempt to fit in, he spent an inordinate amount of time and money trying to be an Englishman. He bought a top hat and tailcoat. In order to gain an appreciation for western music, he bought a violin and hired a music teacher. He also hired an English teacher to help him with his language difficulties.

In the Spring of 1891, Gandhi completed the requirements of his legal studies and became a member of the British bar. Two days later he returned to India.

Legal Career

The voyage back to India was a stormy trip. Upon his arrival, his brother had notified him that their mother had died in his absence. His grief plagued him for years. He saw despair all around him. Instead of treating his loving wife with compassion and peace, he often turned on her in fits of jealousy and rage. He hated the fact that she was so ignorant, but never took the time to teach her how to read and write. At the time Gandhi and his wife Kasturbai's son Harilal was four years old, she was pregnant with their second child.

In his chosen profession of law, Gandhi was not fairing very well. He believed his comical appearance hampered him from getting clients. In their book, Mahatma Gandhi, Doris and Harold Faber wrote about a time when a friend of Gandhi's hired him to represent the friend at court.

As he stood up in the Small Causes Court, his head was reeling. He had prepared his case carefully, but he forgot everything. He could not think of a single word to say; at last, he sat down again. Was the judge laughing at him? In his misery, Gandhi scribbled a note asking his client to engage another lawyer.

His life and legal career were at a low point when he received an offer from a local law firm that was representing a Muslim owned business in South Africa. They needed help and Gandhi needed a change. In April 1893, Gandhi left his wife and two sons in India and he boarded a ship to the British Colony of South Africa.

In South Africa he wore English style clothing and an Indian turban. He suffered many insults and indignities. Many hotels and first class railway compartments were reserved "for Europeans only." In many respects, Gandhi would have suffered from the same type of discrimination that African-Americans felt in the deep South during the early 20th century.

In June 1894, his one-year contract had expired and he was preparing to leave for India. At his farewell party, an Indian friend of Gandhi showed him a newspaper article stating that the Legislative Assembly was considering a Bill to bar Indians the Right to vote. His friend asked him to stay in South Africa and fight the oppression.

Political Career

In July 1894, at the age of 25 and despite his fear of public speaking, he immediately became a political figure to be reckoned with. He settled in Dunbar, South Africa and began to organize the Indian community. He publicized the oppression of Indians in South Africa and had articles published in London, Calcutta and throughout South Africa.

In 1896, Gandhi traveled back to India to bring his wife and sons back to South Africa. He took the opportunity to drum up support for his cause in India. Upon his return to South Africa in January 1897, he was assaulted by a white mob and almost lynched. He refused to press charges against the assailants.

Gandhi refused to hold a grudge and urged people to do what was right. When the Boer War broke out in 1899, instead of Gandhi holding distain for the government that oppressed the Indian community, he urged them to serve their country. He organized an ambulance corps of 1,100 volunteers. After the war, a partnership flourished between the Boers and the British, but the plight of the Indians got worse.

In 1906, a particular oppressive Indian Registration Law was about to be passed. Gandhi organized the Indian population and led the protest. A Pledge was taken to disobey the Law and to suffer whatever penalty was required. This was the beginning of what Gandhi called Satyagraha, which means devotion to truth. This was a new way of protesting wrongs through accepting rather than resisting punishment; instead of inflicting suffering on the wrongdoer, the masses invited the wrongdoers to cause them suffering.

The Indian community suffered, including loss of jobs, floggings, imprisonment and even death, yet they hung together. Finally in 1913, Gandhi negotiated a settlement with South Africa. Gandhi's nonviolent resistance had won the day.

In July 1914, when Gandhi left for India, the chief negotiator for South Africa wrote, "The saint has left our shores. I hope forever."

During his stay in South Africa his spiritual life flourished. He studied many religions including Christianity, Islam, and Hinduism. He found great benefit in these religions, but also saw things that were lacking. He believed that no one religion held all of the answers. In January 1915, he visited a famous Indian poet by the name of Rabindranath Tagore, who had won the Nobel Prize for literature. Upon seeing Gandhi, Tagore cried out, "Mahatma Gandhi!" and the name stuck. "Mahatma" is ancient Sanskrit meaning "the great soul"; it is a title similar in nature to that of "Saint" in the Catholic Church.

Indian Independence

In India, Gandhi at first did not advocate for total independence, but rather for a situation like Canada had at the time. Canada was a dominion of the British Empire and received benefit there from, but Canadians were in charge of the day by day governing of their country. Gandhi said

that the best way to accomplish this, India would need to show its loyalty to the British. Even though he still maintained his nonviolence stance, he encouraged Indians to join the British Army and fight for them in World War I.

Even with the Indian community helping the British, in February 1919, the British enacted the Row Latt Bills, which allowed the British to arrest and imprison Indians on a suspicion of sedition and without trial. Gandhi announced a Satyagraha struggle in India. British Soldiers acted with a heavy hand and killed almost 400 Indians.

By late 1920, Gandhi had more political power than any politician to set foot in the Country. He continued to press and reinforce the program of non-violent non-cooperation with the British. The Indians boycotted anything British including manufactures, courts, schools and offices. The British Responded by arresting Indians by the thousands, who lined up and cheerfully went to jail.

It seemed that Gandhi's movement was unstoppable by the British forces, which it was. However, in February 1922, Gandhi himself called off all civil disobedience in response to a violent outbreak by Indians in a remote village.

Gandhi was arrested on March 10, 1922 and tried for sedition. He received a six-year term and was released in February 1924. Indian unity had broken down while he was in prison and there was waning support for his nonviolent stance. Gandhi then took somewhat of a break from politics.

Gandhi came back stronger that ever, and in March 1930, he launched a Satyagraha against the British Salt Tax. The effort resulted in the arrest of 60,000 people and the British agreed to negotiate. The civil disobedience was called off and Gandhi went to London to negotiate. More or less, it was a double-cross by the British, Gandhi gained little. When he returned to India he was again arrested, and the oppression of Indians increased.

In September 1932, he began a much publicized Fast to end the oppression. Gandhi was released from prison and some reform was obtained.

In 1934, he resigned from his leadership of the Indian Congress Party because he believed that it adopted the policy of nonviolence as a political expedient rather than a fundamental creed. He decided to travel the country helping the poor.

World War II brought about new challenges and opportunities. Gandhi hated Fascism and all it stood for and despised war. Britain was so stressed by World War II, it was in no position to keep an iron fist on India. A British minister came to India and brought an offer that Gandhi did not accept. The British reacted sharply by imprisoning the entire Indian National Congress.

The Members of the Congress were released and Gandhi kept up the pressure on the British. Finally in mid-August 1947, the Mountbatten Plan established Pakistan and India as independent countries. Gandhi's dream of an independent India was finally realized. However, he was always disappointed that the Muslims and Hindus could not have found unity in one country, instead of two.

Gandhi's Legacy

A brief comparison of the life and legacy of Gandhi and Benito Mussolini is interesting, -Both were born approximately the same time; Gandhi in 1869 and Mussolini in 1883; -Both were born into meager surroundings; -Both men were short in stature; -Both emerged as significant political figures in the early 1920's;

-Gandhi taught freedom through pacifism and nonviolence; Mussolini taught conquest and subjugation through a hatred of pacifism and extreme violence;

--Gandhi's name is synonymous with pacifism and nonviolent struggle; Mussolini's name is synonymous with Fascism and war;

-Gandhi's legacy is one of love, peace, compassion, and all that can be right with humanity; Mussolini's legacy is one of hate, violence, disdain, and all that can go wrong with humanity.

It is this compassion that should be taught in our schools. The youth of the world must understand the difference between the actions of these men. The Holy Writ tells us that set before us is good and evil, life and death, and it is up to us to choose. We must choose life, love and peace and teach our children to do the same. The life, times, and actions of Gandhi and Mussolini can be a major aid toward completion of this goal.

NICOLO MACHIAVELLI

The term "Machiavellian" is used to describe someone who is crafty, sly, deceitful, or cunning. The pejorative term was first used by the French in the 16th century and is a direct reference to Nicolo Machiavelli.

Machiavelli was born on May 3, 1469 in Florence, Italy. He died 58 years later on June 21, 1527 in the same city. His love for the city of Florence is evident from his writing. His greatest work, *Ilprincipe* (The Prince), brought him fame and the reputation of amoral cynicism. He is remembered fondly in the northern Italian city as one of the greatest writers in Italian history, an honorable statesman, Florentine patriot, philosopher and original political terrorist. **Background and Formative Years**

Nicolo Machiavelli was born into one of the most prominent and wealthy families in the important city of Florence. The Machiavelli family was a political force to be reckoned with since the 13th century. The Machiavelli name was respected and honored throughout Italy. Nicolo's father however, was by no means one of the wealthy Machiavelli's. In fact, he may well have been the poorest member of the powerful family. He owned a small amount of property outside the city which yielded a very meager income. He was also a lawyer. However, he was restricted in the practice of law because he was prohibited from holding any public office because he was deemed by the Florentine courts as an "insolent debtor of the commune." Accordingly, the practice of law had to be done on almost a clandestine basis and a very limited source of additional income. The family had to live

frugally and to a much lower standard than most of their relatives with the same surname. Years later Nicolo would write that he had "Learnt to do without before he learnt to enjoy."

Nicolo's aristocratic "peers" went to the best schools and studied Latin and Greek. They filled the lecture halls of the most famous instructors of the day. However, due to the poor estate of the young Nicolo, he was unable to attain the educational levels of the aristocratic youth. He never studied Greek, and according to his father's memories, Nicolo learned more by self-studying than in school. His father further stated that he studied Latin under obscure teachers and on his own.

Many scholars believe that it was Machiavelli's lack of a more fundamental education that allowed him to break out of "philosophic mold of the time. Instead of parroting the thoughts of the teaching intellectual elite, Nicolo's thinking was original and his style or writing unique. **Political Career**

At the age of 29, Machiavelli was named the head of the second chancery in the Florentine government. His appointment was made possible due to a change in the Florentine Government. An ascetic monk named Savonarola was extremely outspoken and tried to impose religious and political reforms on the government. His efforts got him executed and changes in the Florentine government ensued, opening the way for the triumph of an opposing faction, of which Machiavelli was an active member.

He was relatively unknown, and although the position he was appointed to did not carry substantial power, it was no less an important one. Initially, his position was limited to internal affairs of the state, but it was subsequently merged with the executive counsel,

known as the / *Diece,* (The Ten). He was also appointed secretary to the magistracy, which, through the executive counsel, directed foreign affairs and defense.

In 1500, Machiavelli was sent on a diplomatic mission to France, which had a significant impact on his political philosophy. On the trip he saw first hand how a powerful nation operates under the rule and authority of a monarchy. This "single prince" Rule would be contemplated by Nicolo and occupy much of his thinking.

When he traveled back to Florence, he found himself in the midst of political turmoil. The republic stood to be ruined by the ambitious Cesare Borgia, who was trying to establish a state for himself in central Italy. During this period, Nicolo was repeatedly sent on diplomatic missions. He would later write that he relished in the danger and hardship of the missions. It was at this time that he wrote *Del modo di trattar e i Sudditi della Val di Chiana ribellati* ("On the Way to Deal with the Rebel Subjects of the Valdichiana.")

In "On the Way..." which was written in 1503, Nicolo detailed a new doctrine: "The world has always been inhabited by human beings who have always had the same passions." During this period, he traveled twice to meet with Cesare Borgia on diplomatic missions. On December 31, 1502, he personally witnessed the brutal massacre by Cesare of his rebellious captains in the Italian town of Sinigaglia. In response to this Nicolo wrote his famous short work entitled, Descrizone del modo tenuto dal Duca Valentino nello Ammazzare Citellozzo... ("On the Manner Adopted by the Duke Valentino to Kill Vitellozzo...") It was clear from this item that the whole violent episode caught his imagination.

Machiavelli knew that Italy was in a desperate circumstance with abject poverty, ineffective government with no resolution in sight. He was intrigued how Cesare Borgia could have conquered and created a state for himself in such a short period of time. Nicolo studied Cesare's methods including violence, cunning and well defined goals. Machiavelli believed that Italy could only be saved by a prince with the same qualities and attributes as he witnessed in Cesare.

However, Nicolo's admiration was not for the man Cesare, but for the idealization of his methods. It was this idealization of a savior prince that could swoop in and rescue the Italy from all of its ills that consumed his thinking.

In 1503, Pope Alexander VI, who was the father of Cesare Borgia, died. His immediate successor, Pope Pius III, himself died in short order. Machiavelli was then sent to Rome as a representative from Florence to the papal conclave which elected Pope Julius II. This new Pope was a staunch enemy of Cesare Borgia and his entire family.

The political power of the Pope in the 17th century could not be denied and the fates of Nicolo's hero Cesare's days were numbered. Initially, Nicolo was distraught over the decline of Cesare, but unable to miss an opportunity, celebrated the imprisonment of his idol. Machiavelli would write that Cesare's imprisonment was proper, "Which he deserved as a rebel against Christ." The Christian ethic of Machiavelli did not manifest itself while Cesare's father was the Pope, but only after Rome targeted Cesare.

When Machiavelli returned to Florence he was pleased to find that another of his heroes, Piero Soderini, had been elected chief magistrate for life. Nicolo began to immediately curry favor with Soderini and soon became the chief magistrate's right-hand man.

Nicolo's influence and power rapidly increased and he decided to use his power to establish and control a military. He had been studying military affairs for years and was convinced that conventional wisdom was incorrect as far as military matters were concerned. He observed that the common practice at the time was for states of Italy to hire mercenary troops to fight their battles. He noted that these troops were expensive, untrained, undisciplined and extremely arrogant. He contrasted this with his observations in France of the benefits of a professional state military, his extensive study of Ancient Roman military matters, and his first-hand observation of the improvement of the military when Cesare Borgin replaced mercenary forces with his own military.

Machiavelli began to ardently lobby for the establishment of a militia for the Florentine state. There was much resistance from the Florentine population as well as the administrators of the state. Nicolo carried the day, and in 1505 the chief magistrate agreed to an experiment to establish a small military force. The idea gained acceptance and the following year a counsel of nine was created to control the military. Machiavelli was appointed as secretary of this counsel. He divided the state into two military districts and would personally inspect the troops and their training. In addition to these duties, Nicolo's responsibilities at the chancery were increasing and he was the chief magistrate's trusted envoy in important matters. In 1506, he was sent on a mission to Pope Julius II, whose papal armies were formidable and were on the move to suppress those forces contrary to his own.

In late 1507, Maximilian I, the Holy Roman Emperor was planning to invade Italy from Germany in the North. The chief magistrate sent his most trusted subordinate, Nicolo, on a spy mission to Switzerland and Germany to assess the threat. The day after his return, on June 17, 1508, Machiavelli wrote the famous document *Rapporto delle cose della* Magna ("Report on the State of Germany").

Machiavelli wrote with great understanding and insight on the strengths and political weaknesses of the German nation. His writings also included his theories of the situation and not just a factual account.

About this time the citystate of Pisa freed itself from the rule of the Florentines. After his return from Germany, Nicolo was authorized to lead his newly created militia into Pisa to regain control. He was advised by administrators in Florence to remain in the city instead of traveling with the troops. He disregarded their advice and said that he needed to be leading his troops to victory. On June 8, 1509, Pisa gave up its quest for independence and acceded to Florentine rule. Machiavelli and the Florentine militia received much praise and increased status for this victory.

Machiavelli's euphoria was short-lived. In July of 1510, Maximilian was threatening another invasion and Florence's ally, Louis XII of France was talking war with Pope Julius II. The Florentines were well aware that if they were drawn into a war with the papal army they would lose. Nicolo traveled to France to try and get Louis XII to make peace with the Pope. Machiavelli made no headway and returned to Florence convinced that there would be a war between France and the papal army, and that Florence would be dragged into it. He immediately began to firm up the Florentine military machine.

In the late summer of 1511, Nicolo traveled one more time to see their French ally, to

ask him to discontinue supporting a rogue faction of malcontents in Pisa. This time the king agreed because he acknowledged that his actions brought the wrath of Pope Julius II upon Florence.

Upon his return from France, Machiavelli immediately traveled to Pisa to disband the rogue faction, which he accomplished without incident. This was perhaps his finest military hour. The rejoicing was short lived. The Pope's army was already marching toward Florence to punish the state for daring to defy the Pope. Chief Magistrate Soderini was removed from Power and the Medici returned to once again rule Florence.

Under New Management

As soon as the Medici took over, Machiavelli was fired from his position and forbidden to enter politics. In 1513, a conspiracy to depose the Medici was uncovered, and Machiavelli's name was mentioned. Nicolo was thrown into prison; tortured and abused, but maintained his innocence. The conspirators further implicated him; he was finally released under tight restrictions.

At this time Pope Julius II died and the papacy was given to Giovanni de' Medici under the name Pope Leo X. In order to curry favor with Pope Leo X (Medici), Nicolo composed a song in honor of the new Pope. The song entitled "Canto degli spiriti beati" (Song of the Blessed Spirits") failed to impress the Medici. Machiavelli was reduced to poverty and forced to reside on a small property outside the city that he inherited from his father. It was during this extended free time that he wrote his two famous works, *Ilprincipe* ("The Prince"), and *Discorsi sopra la prima deca di Tito Livio* ("Discourses on the First Ten Books of Livy").

Machiavelli longed for the days for power and adventure. He dreamed about a "new prince" who would return Florence to its proper estate. He knew that the person who would rise up and redeem Florence would need to be powerful and firm. In "The Prince"

and "Discourses", Nicolo discussed the techniques necessary for the seizure and retention of power. He exalted "reasons of state" and discounted morality. Whether or not Machiavelli should receive any credit, renaissance diplomacy for the next century conformed to his writings.

There is little doubt that Machiavelli was driven by a desire to see a unified Italy. He believed that once the country was united by a "new prince", there would then be time for the advancement of virtue and morality. Nicolo wrote that even religion must not be made into a tool for the state.

Even though the term was not used until after his death, Nicolo was credited as the originator of the "reason of state." He knew that some of the concepts in his writings were controversial and written to generate reaction. He further said that certain of his cynical precepts would not need to have been written if man were not so wicked. He wrote that he longed for a society of good pure men, and admired less advanced societies as being less corrupt.

"The Prince" was dedicated to Lorenzo de'Medici, who ruled Florence at the time. However, Lorenzo was not impressed and did not appoint Nicolo to a position that would allow him to feed his family.

It was during this period that Machiavelli wrote a comedy entitled La Mandragola ("The Mandrake"), in which the corruption and wickedness of men are reduced to laughter. This writing also attacked the church and clergy that he resented for the loss of his political position.

Second Political Career

Machiavelli's continual attempts to court Lorenzo's favor never materialized. It was not until Lorenzo's death that his fortunes began to change. Cardinal Giulio de' Medici began to rule Florence and agreed to have Nicolo elected as the official historian of Florence. In November 1520, as the official historian he received an annual salary of 57 gold florins. He excelled at this job and his salary was increased to 100 florins and he was allowed to make additional funds through part-time work.

One of Nicolo's additional projects was to compose a discourse for Pope Leo X and the organization of the Florentine government after the death of Lorenzo. In this work, he strongly recommended that the Pope restore Florence to its former liberties. Several months later, Pope Leo X died.

Cardinal Giulio de' Medici continued to govern Florence and was firm on his desire to reform the government. Giulio hired Nicolo to advise him on reforms. Machiavelli reworked the discourse he wrote for Pope Leo X and presented it to Giulio, who was impressed with Nicolo's work.

In September 1521, Pope Adrian VI died and Machiavelli's benefactor, Giulio de' Medici became Pope Clement VII. Nicolo was now writing directly for the Pope in writing the history of Florence. In June, 1525, he presented the Pope with eight volumes, which impressed the Pope. In return Nicolo received 120 florins and was encouraged to keep writing. In the *Istorie Florentine* (History of Florence") he was understandably more interested in political correctness which would not offend his benefactors than in historical accuracy.

In April, 1527 Nicolo was elected secretary to a committee in charge of Fortifications. He then worked with the papal army against the Holy Roman Emperor Charles V. This continued until the Emperor's forces sacked Rome in May 1527 and brought the war to an end.

Florence had regained its freedom from the Medici and Machiavelli returned to Florence hoping that he would be reinstated to the position he had before the Medici took over. The new leaders of Florence barred Machiavelli from holding office. Nicolo fell into a depression, became ill and less than one month later on June 22, 1527, he died.

Legacy

Machiavelli was a good father to his five children and loved Florence, "more than his own soul." He has been credited with being one of the founders of the philosophy of history. In his philosophical thought, he knew that he was moving down "a road as yet untrodden by man."

Building on the principle that human nature does not change, he originated the idea of historical cycles. He sought to escape from transcendent reason and transcendent will toward the empirical. He did this through the thoughts and observation of a man not tainted by a strict university education and no specific philosophical or religious preconceptions. He was seeking, "What a principality is, the variety of such states, how they are won, how they are held, how they are lost."

In today's philosophical and intellectual environment his views would not seem very radical, but in the early 16th century, they were most remarkable. It would take almost another 100 years before Francis Bacon picked up the mantle and carried on Machiavelli's work. It was in Bacon's advancement of learning that Machiavelli's work was taken to the next level.

Most scholars do not believe that the Renaissance produced any great moral philosophers; however, Machiavelli is viewed as having historical significance in the history of ethics. The importance on ethics of Machiavelli's "The Prince" is that it ignored the established ethics norms. He wrote," it is necessary for a prince, who wishes to maintain himself, to learn how not to be good, and how to use this knowledge and not use it, according to the necessities of the case."

Some scholars maintain that Machiavelli's writings were an attempt to satirize the actions of the princely rulers of Italy during the Renaissance. Others viewNicolo as a political scientist, listing how political power is maintained and what human beings are like, writing without passing moral judgment.

Regardless of what the intentions of Nicolo were, the name Machiavelli will remain synonymous with cyniqism, cunningness, and deceit.

/ "Indivisible
Democracy" /
Gangstaz, Ballaz, Shot callers, Robbers, Murderers
Red, white & blue, Suit & tie policy makers. I'm talking 'bout Lawyers turn mayors,
Mayors turn Governors, Presidential election-jackin'-Sons & Fathers,
United Nations war-mongers. Skull & Bone puppet-masters,
Clean shaven & comb-overs, Church going, tax collecting, Merry Christmas wishing,
Duck hunting executioners1
Whatever you're selling, they want in!!
NAFTA regulations increase profits by the millions, Off tarrifs & embargos,
On everything, from food to clothes! Whatever you're pushing, they want in!
Opium, diamonds, oil, weed or coke, They want a cut. Or else; Family, village, and whole countries
if necessary.
Going down in a blaze of glory & up in a puff of smoke!!
This ain't new! This is History & legacy!
From Hiroshima naypom memory, To hell-fire missiles,
Simultaneously disseminating Afghani & Iraqie!! Globalization, world domination, and
Secret Societies, Inbreeding with Monarchies,
Rewriting & dictating foreign policies.
No grease, watch 'em
Raw dog, Penetrate, ejaculate and violate.
Miss Geneva's Convention! Stay on course,
Complete the mission "We're going after weapons of mass destruction,
Tell 'em Colon Powell!
The Title Song is
"War on Terrorism" Track One,
U.S. led invasions. Democrat & Republican parties, Different styles - same patterns,
Cuz it's, ONE NATION Indivisible,
Appear to be separate, but actually,
Interconnected like "Crop Circle formations." For your information, from the era of
industrialization,
To the present. Contract bids of privatization; The rich get richer, and the poor get poor-er
How do you spell HALIBURTON??
                              C-A-P-I-T-A-L-I-S-M!!!!!
Sounds like a bunch of rhetoric?
The words of an uneducated fool talking crazy?
Tell me....Who? When & Where in the world,
Have you ever seen muthafuckaz Steal Energy???
I ain't talking 'bout no extension cord.
House-to-house-junction-box-kilowatts,
I'm talking 'bout
State to State "rolling blackouts!!
From New York to Connecticut, Chicago to Ohio,
Texas to Vegas, and across to Cali,

Shuttin' down power grids
Jackin' electricity!
Enron hollering.....
"Fuck You --Pay Me"!!
Bush & Chaney laughing, as their homey Ken Lehay robbed PSE&G,
Stuck up his own Company,
Filed for Bankruptcy, got indicted -- found guilty.
Biggest fraud case in U.S. history,
Had a heart-attack & died.
The day before he was to be sent
To the penitentiary....Allegedly!
CEO of Enron -- major contributor to the
Bush-Chaney presidential campaign...in the penitentiary
Yeah, he had a heart-attack & died the day before aiight,
Hocus-pocus, like Mr. Machiavelli!!!
Is anyone paying attention to the fuckery
Being brought to you by: "In Your Face Productions,"
In association with: "New World Order,"
Hosted by: "illuminati!"

Indivisible Democracy.